The

Devotion

to the

Holy Face

at St. Peter's of the Vatican & in Other Celebrated Places

Rev. Abbe Janvier

SENSUS FIDELIUM PRESS

Gastonia, North Carolina

ARCHBISHOPRIC OF TOURS

I very willingly authorize the publication of the work entitled: *The Devotion to **the** Holy Face,* which cannot but contribute to the glory of our Lord and the sanctification of the faithful.

CHARLES, *Archbishop of Tours.*

Tours, 16th Nov. 1883.

CERTIFICATE OF THE PICTURES OF THE HOLY FACE BROUGHT FROM ROME

(Latin text.)

SACROSANCTAE BASILICAE
PRINCIPIS APOSTOLORUM DE URBE
CANONICUS

Universis praesentes litteras inspecturis fidem facio, ac testor me imaginem Vultus DOMINI NOSTRI JESU CHRISTI, ad inatar Sanctissimi Sudarii Veronicae in tela albi coloris impressam, altitudinis ... unciarum, lotitudinis ... unc., reverenter applicasse eidom Sudario, nee non Ligno vivificae Crucis et Lanceae Dominicae cuspidi, quae **in** praedicia nostra Basilica religiosissime asservatur, ac pluribus Summorum Pontificum Diplomatibus, maximaque populorum vencratione celebrantur. In quorum fidem praedictom Imaginem et has praesentes litteras meo sigillo obsignavi, et subscripsi.

Datum ex aedibus meis, die 21 Junii MDCCCLXVI.

Indictione Rom... 9. Pontificatus Smi D. N. Domini Pii Papa IX, Pont Max. anno XXI.

(L. s.)   A. **THEODOLI.**

(English TRANSLATION.)

I, CANON OF THE VERY HOLY BASILICA
OF THE PRINCE OF THE APOSTLES AT ROME

I certify and I attest to all those who shall behold these present, that a picture or the Face or OUR LORD JESUS Cl/RIST, similar to the Most Holy Veil of Veronica printed upon cloth white in colour... inches high and... inches wide has been respectfully applied by mo **to** the said Veil, as well as **to** the wood of the vivifying Cross and to the spear or the Lance of Our Lord which are religiously preserved in our above named Basilica, and rendered celebrated by several diplomas or the Sovereign Pontiffs and by the great veneration or the people. In faith or which I have sealed with my seal the said Image and those presents, and I have signed.

Given In my palace, the 21st or Juno or the year of Our Lord **1866.** Roman Indiction 9, and in the Pontifi**cate** of His Holiness Pius IX., year **XXI.**

(Place of the seal.)   **A.**

THEODOLI.

THE TRUE COPY

OF THE

Holy Face of Our Lord Jesus Christ

which is preserved and venerated
very religiously at Rome, in the Basilica of Saint Peter at the
Vatican.

Multi dicunt: Quis ostendii nobis bona? Signatum est s**uper** nos
lumen Vultus tui, Domine. (Ps. IV, 7.)

Many say- "Who **sheweth us** good things? The light of thy
Countenance, O Lord**, is** signed upon us; **thou hast** given gladness
in **my heart. "**

IMAGO TRIVMPHALIS TITULI
VIVIFICÆ CRUCIS
DOMINI NOSTRI JESU CHRISTI
QUALIS HODIE ROMÆ CONSPICITUR

Title of the Cross

A solis ortu usque ad occasum, * *laudabile Nomen Domini.* (Ps. cxii, 3.)

From the rising of the sun unto the going down of the same, * the Name of the Lord is worthy of praise.

PREFACE

A simple abridgment of the story of the "Veronica" of the Vatican
is no longer sufficient to satisfy the pious curiosity of the reader.
For now, the friend of the Holy Face ardently desires to be made
acquainted with everything that relates to a devotion, the progress of
which becomes every day more striking. Other analogous subjects, no
less interesting, deserve to attract his attention; it is therefore our wish
to give a sketch of some amongst them.

During long centuries, Flanders and Hainault, situated on the
borders of France and Belgium, united in offering public worship
to an ancient picture which was a copy of the one at Rome. It was
styled the Holy Face of Montreuil-les-Dames, now transferred to
Notre-Dame de Laon. Three towns in catholic Spain, Jaen, Osa de la
Vega and Alicante, have possessed from time immemorial celebrated
pictures of the Holy Face which have been the objects of public
veneration. Three years ago, the archiepiscopal city of Lucca, in
Tuscany, solemnized by a triduum of splendid feasts, which were
at once religious and secular in character, the eleventh centenary of
the Volto Santo, which the people look upon as their joy and their
treasure.

It has seemed to us that the servants of the Holy Face, who earnestly
desire to follow the example set them by M. Dupont in glorifying the

divine Effigy of the crucified Christ, ought not to remain ignorant of what took place in former ages and of what still occurs at the present day in these memorable localities. Above all it is well they should thoroughly understand that the devotion which they practice with so much ardor is not a new idea to the Church; that it has existed at all times and everywhere; that it dales from the origin of Christianity; and that, in many places, respecting which we are far too ignorant, it has had its sanctuaries, its altars, its feasts, its confraternities, its pilgrimages, its processions, and its different institutions, according to the character of the people and in conformity with what was required in varying circumstances.

It is these incidents, therefore, with which this little book will make our readers acquainted, not by means of reasoning or discussion, but through the teaching of history and the recital of facts.

Our small volume is composed of eight different notices devoted to the Holy Face of the Vatican, - the Holy Face of Montreuil-sous-Laon, - the Holy Face of Jaen, - the Holy Face of Osa de la Vega, - the Holy Face of Alicante, - the Holy Face of Lucca, - the Holy Face of Tours, - and the Holy Face of Edessa.

In order that these modest pages might be compiled with a view to the utmost possible accuracy, we have had recourse to documents, printed or in manuscript, obtained from the localities themselves and which have been supplied to us by competent persons. Kind hands have moreover helped us to draw them up. To avoid the too great multiplication of notes at the bottom of the pages, we have added to each recital a summary account of the principal sources, to which we have had recourse.

It will be easily perceived that we have not given to the subject the amplification suitable to it; to do so, volumes would have been necessary. Many other pictures of the Holy Face, and innumerable other portraits of Our Lord are equally worthy of respect and of study. But to keep within due limits, we have by preference chosen those which seemed to be the most closely connected with the works of reparation practiced in the Oratory at Tours. Our object will have been attained, if our pious readers, rejoicing in and encouraged by the great examples and the marvels of grace of which they have perhaps been hitherto ignorant, should feel themselves to be more than ever determined to invoke in their needs the sorrowful Face of our Lord, and to offer to it fervent acts of faith and of expiation in compensation for the outrages inflicted upon it at the present day.

P. JANVIER.

CONTENTS

1. The Holy Face of the Vatican   1

2. The Holy Face of Montreuil-Sous-Laon   38

3. The Holy Face of Jaen   49

4. The Holy Face of Osa de la Vega   58

5. The Holy Face of Alicante   65

6. The Holy Face of Lucca   69

7. The Holy Face of Tours   80

8. The Holy Face of Edessa   86

9. Conclusion   88

10. Chapter 10   90

11. Prayers in Honor of the Holy Face   91

12. Prayers to the Holy Face   102

13. Promises Made by Our Lord to Those Who Worship The Holy Face   105

14. Conditions Necessary in Order to Become An Associate   110

15. Notices   115

THE HOLY FACE OF THE VATICAN

The worship of the Holy Face of our Lord Jesus Christ, as approved at Rome, and as practiced throughout the Church, began on Calvary. It dates from that pious woman whose remembrance has been attached, from time immemorial, to the sixth station of the Cross, and which tradition agrees to call by the name of Veronica. Before recounting the heroic act, which has rendered her so celebrated and describing the worship which has for its object the miraculous imprint made upon her veil, we think that it will be useful to retrace, in a few words, the story of her life. We shall then state how the relic left by her to the Roman Pontiffs has been honored in the church of St. Peter at the Vatican, and religiously preserved down to the present day.

I

The name of Veronica is not to be found anywhere in the Gospels; hut in all probability the woman so designated is no other than the one of whom St. Luke speaks (ch. viii., 43, 48). He represents her to us as afflicted, for twelve years, with an issue of blood which no physician had been able to heal. But "she came behind Jesus, and touched the hem of His garment," and felt immediately that she was cured. After the question put to her by the Savior, and which gave her an opportunity to proclaim her belief in His power, she deserved to hear His divine mouth pronounce the words- "My daughter, thy faith has saved thee; depart in peace."

Trustworthy authors affirm the identity of this fervent Israelite with Veronica. Their opinion is founded upon a document taken from three very ancient Missals- firstly that of Milan called the Ambrosian Missal, secondly the one entitled the Missal of Jaen, in Spain, and thirdly the Missal of Aosta. In this document, in the mass of the feast, which is fixed for the 4th of February, St. Veronica, who wiped the Face of our Lord, is invoked in the prayers, the divine Picture is adored in the Prose, and the Gospel is the very one in which St. Luke relates the cure of the sick woman1.

"It is probable," Father Ventura remarks with regard to this subject, "that she who received from the Savior the distinguished favor of wiping with her own bands the sweat and blood from His divine Face, is the same woman who touched His garment with an heroic faith, and, in so doing, rendered a most beautiful testimony to His divinity."

Full of gratitude, the happy Israelite so miraculously cured, devoted her life to the service of her liberator. She attached herself to the footsteps of Jesus, and followed Him together with Mary Magdalen, and the other holy women of Judea who accompanied the divine Master and assisted Him in His material needs, whilst He went with His apostles from town to town, from village to village, preaching the Gospel, and announcing the Kingdom of God. She was with the Savior, it appears, on Palm Sunday, when he made His triumphal entry into Jerusalem; it is even supposed that she had the courage to appear before Pilate, and, together with several other witnesses of His miracles, to make a deposition in His favor.

The greater portion of the historical details which follow have been taken from the Histoire de sainte Veronique, apoire de l'Aquitai11e, and from the remarkable work of Msgr. Cirot de la VIiie, Canon of Bordeaux, as inserted in the Petits Bollandistes (3rd of February).

It is, at any rate, incontestable that she went to meet him on the path to Calvary. A modern historian, Dr. Sepp, recounts the tradition in this manner- "A woman named Berenice or Veronica draws near to Jesus with a compassionate expression on her countenance, and with a handkerchief wipes His Face covered with sweat, in such a manner that the adorable Face remains imprinted on it with its bleeding features."

And here is a more detailed account of the same event as given by the erudite Piazza and other equally learned authors- "After Jesus had quitted the praetorium of Pilate, laden with His Cross, and covered with the blood issuing from the wounds he had received during the flagellation and from the Crown of thorns, and had proceeded four hundred and fifty steps on the path to Calvary, He approached a house which stood at the corner of the street"[1] . Veronica then, perceiving Him from afar, came, full of compassion, to meet Him, and having removed the veil which she wore on her head, she presented it to Him that he might make use of it to wipe His Face, all bathed as it was with blood and sweat. Christ, having benignantly received it at her hands, gave it back to her afterwards, leaving upon it, as a gracious recompense, the impress of His holy Face. The resemblance was so complete, that it is even possible to perceive the mark made by the hand which dealt Him a sacrilegious blow. Rejoicing over the

---

1. Others say "the house or Veronica" which was on the road to Calvary. The site was purchased by the Greek Catholics from the Turks in the year 1883.

possession of so precious a treasure, the illustrious lady preserved it in her house with jealous care.

Her traditional name of "Veronica" would seem to have had its origin in this memorable action. Its meaning is "Victorious," and it is composed of two Greek words which signify "I obtain the victory." The glorious epithet of "Pheronique," or Veronica, is frequently met with in the odes of Pindar, who, employing it in the masculine gender, applies it to the victor in the Olympian games. Certain Greek historians also use it in the feminine gender as the designation of illustrious princesses or celebrated towns. It passed from thence into the Christian history of the first centuries of the Church, where it is attributed to saints, to virgins and to martyrs of different countries. The Latins, in transferring it to their language, most probably gave it to the Jewish woman of whom we have spoken, at the time when she came to the West.

Certain learned men of the last century have endeavored to form the name in question from the Latin word vera, true, joined to the Greek word icon, image (true image)- in this way endeavoring to appropriate to a person, in the quality of a proper name, the name and the quality of the "image."

This hybrid combination does violence to all the laws of philology and is not worthy of acceptation. On the other hand, the etymology which we have adopted is much more natural and agrees perfectly well with the rules of language and the data of history. It is true that sometimes the name of a thing is given to a person, and that, speaking, for example, of the pictures of the Holy Face, we call them "Veronicas;" but the name itself, the personal name of Veronica, belongs to the holy woman in question, and will forever remain hers as a testimony to the everlasting and pious gratitude rendered to her, by posterity, for her heroic conduct towards the Savior on the path to Calvary.

One of our old ascetic authors, full of admiration for this sublime act of Veronica, does not hesitate to place it above even the most sublime examples of virtue which the world has ever witnessed. "Heroic woman," he exclaims, "thou art incomparable, thou hast no equal upon earth! At the very time when the whole universe conspired together against the life of its Savior; at the very moment when God the Father abandoned Him into the hands of sinners, and when the angels of peace wept bitterly over Him, without being able to give Him any succor; at the very hour when the apostles forsook, betrayed and denied Him; at the very time when His dear mother, the blessed Virgin, by fainting away had profoundly afflicted Him; at the very time when the whole of the city of Jerusalem demanded His death and crucifixion; at the very time when it was a crime and a sacrilege for the Jews to recognize in Him a holy man, thou didst revere Him as thy Messiah, thou didst adore Him as thy God , thou gavest Him refreshment and consolation in the midst of his greatest enemies. Thou didst, of a truth, merit an immortality of glory both in time and in eternity, and, therefore, the Savior made thee the most precious gift which he has ever bestowed on any earthly creature, for He gave thee His portrait impressed on thy veil. Spread it then in sight of the four portions of the globe; make all men behold the piteous and disfigured Face of a suffering God. Preach by means of the holy Effigy the passion of Jesus Christ and make it to reach far beyond the places to which the apostles extended the knowledge of it. As for me, I promise that I will venerate thee during the whole of my life, because of this heroic act of thy charity, and, whether living or dying, I will bear in mind the remembrance and in my mouth the name of the incomparable Veronica[2]."

An author of the seventeenth century contemplates Jesus bearing His cross, and addresses Him in these words- "Why is it not permitted to me, oh Jesus, to gather. up all the blood which Thou didst shed when going to Calvary, or why could I not at least treasure in my bosom the drops which the pious Veronica collected in her veil?... Oh, happy Veronica, how richly you were recompensed for the compassion yon showed for my divine Savior! Hardly had you wiped away the blood, the sweat and the tears which ran down His Face, than He left upon your veil the impress of His adorable features, to show us that He gave Himself to you in gratitude for your zeal, and to teach us that He gives Himself to those who, imitating you, assist Him in the person of the afflicted. Happy Veronica, whose ready help was not less agreeable to Jesus Christ than that of Simon, though it might have seemed less useful, but He looks only at our intention in all that we do for Him.

"How good art Thou, divine Redeemer! Thou wert willing to be assisted by a woman as well as by a man, to show us that no one is exempt from a participation in Thy Passion; and also to teach us that Thou bast regard to the delicacy and weakness of even the feeblest amongst us, and that, in order to please Thee, it is sufficient to pity Thy sufferings, and with St. Veronica to feel them in our hearts, when we cannot share them with Simon the Cyrenean, or bear the marks of them on our body like St. Paul. It was Thy love, oh my God, which impressed a semblance of Thy Face upon the veil of Veronica, that thou mightest gain her heart; it was Thy love which, to recompense

---

2. P. Parvilliers, la. Devotion des Predestines, on les Stations de Jerusalem et du Calvaire.

and at the same time to satisfy the tenderness she had conceived for Thee, gave to her Thy heart, so to say, with Thy Face, that she might know that Thy charity was the cause of Thy sufferings, and that she might feed her love for Thee by gazing upon Thee, even during Thy absence.

"Yes, my Savior, Thou didst give Thyself to Veronica on her veil, that she might have joy in Thee spite of Thy absence, in the same manner, almost, that Thou dost give Thyself to believing souls, through faith, which, like a sacred veil, covers the eyes of reason, that by means of it they may behold Thee and consider Thee as in a figure, during this life until they possess Thee really in eternity[3]."

The place where the act performed.by Veronica took place has been venerated as much as the name of the heroic woman. Bernard de Breydenbach, Dean of Mayence, states that "he traversed, on the 14th of July 1483, the long road by which Christ was led from the palace of Pilate to the place of crucifixion, and that he passed before the house of Veronica, which was five hundred and fifty steps distant from the palace of Pilate." Adrichomius of Cologne describes the localities with still greater precision. "The house of Veronica," he says, "stands at the corner of a street... From the place where she met the Christ to the Judiciary gate, where He fell for the second time beneath His cross, He had traversed a space of three hundred and sixty-six steps and eleven feet."

In a bull of the 16th of the calends of August 1561, Pius IV "confirms and ratifies the indulgences inscribed on a very beautiful tablet kept near the Holy Sepulcher of our Lord Jesus Christ".

---

3. Les sentiments du vrai chretien sur la Passion de Jesus-Christ, 1679.

Sixtus V, Benedict XIII, Gregory XVI, successively recognized and published them. Now, upon this tablet, in the nomenclature of holy places to which these indulgences are attached we read- "In the house of St. Veronica there are seven years and as many quarantines". Consequently, this station has been preserved in the exercise known by the name of "The Way of the Cross." The Holy See, being questioned on the subject, declared that under no pretext whatever is permission given to modify the stations, and the tablet which is published thus determines the sixth in the following manner- Verornica wipes the Face of Jesus. Now, where is the church which has not its Way of the Cross, and which does not thus present Veronica before the sight of all men as a model of reparation and a powerful advocate with the sorrowful Face of Jesus?

The miraculous veil, impressed with the features of Jesus, could not be allowed to remain as private property. It was a gift of Jesus Christ to his Church, a relic destined for the center of catholicity. Therefore, Veronica took it to Rome. On account of its importance and of the curious incidents attached to it, this fact claims special study.

It is in this manner that the learned authors Philip of Bergamo and Piazza recount the event.

"Veronica was summoned to depart from Jerusalem and to go to Rome with the Sudarium of Jesus Christ, at this epoch, by order of Caesar and by the intervention of Volusian, a valiant soldier and well known at court. The Emperor was confined to his bed with serious illness. He had been informed by Pilate of the great marvels wrought by Jesus, and he had sent ambassadors to Judea in the hope of obtaining a cure. The messengers found that Jesus had been already crucified. When the Jews sought to deceive them by relating the fable of His body having been carried away by His disciples, Veronica contradicted their falsehoods, and, showing the messengers the impression of His most Holy Face upon her veil, offered to go with them to Rome, promising that, on seeing it, the Emperor would be cured. Having then placed the precious veil in a reliquary, she embarked with the ambassadors, and arrived at Rome, where she was presented to the Emperor. As soon as he had received the holy woman, and had touched the effigy of the Christ, he was completely cured. In consequence of this miracle, Veronica was held in great esteem by the Emperor. "

Sandini gives the same recital in his *History of the Holy Family*, and describes the malady with which the Emperor was afflicted. It was leprosy. This miracle is also related by Ferrari in his *Catalogue of the Saints of Italy*.

However astonishing the fact may appear, it very clearly explains what trustworthy historians, such as Eusebius, Paul Orosius and others, say of the conduct of Tiberius with regard to Jesus Christ and His religion. Informed, they relate, by Pilate of the death, of the resurrection and of the miracles of this extraordinary man, the Emperor desired to place Him amongst his gods. The Senate, they add, irritated at not having been first informed, as was their right, by the Roman governor of his intention, and angry at not having been even consulted by the Emperor, rejected the proposition and decreed the extermination of the Christians. Tiberius revenged himself by menacing with extreme torture whoever should denounce them, and by condemning to death or exile all the senators; with the exception of only two amongst them. He limited himself, however, to raising a statue to the Savior in the interior of his palace, in the place called the "Lararium" where the household gods styled Lares were honored. With regard to the officer in the Emperor's service who was charged with the mission of bringing Veronica to Rome, the author of *Flowers of the Saints*, as well as Philip of Bergamo, call him Volusian, and the

prefaces of the Ambrosian Missal, when mentioning his name, add
that be also was healed of an infirmity of long standing by means
of the miraculous veil. "Mention was formerly made of him, says
Sualdi, in the church at Milan, on the feast of St. Veronica, which was
solemnized on the 4th of February. On that day, remembrance was
made of Veronica and Volusian, not only in the canonical hours; but
also in the mass, which contained a special preface where Volusian was
mentioned. The same personage is also represented in the pictures of
modern date, it is true, which at the present day ornament the crypt
of St. Peter's at Rome. He is moreover spoken of in two ancient books
contained in the library of the Vatican. In the first, written at the time
of Pope Alexander II, in 1160, it is stated that Volusian was a friend
of Tiberius, and that, sent by him to Jerusalem, he bad brought back
Veronica and the Sudarium.

Whoever may have been, however, the ambassador, he only plays a
secondary part here. The main fact, that is to say the translation of the
Holy Face, is attributed to Veronica by the most trustworthy authors,
notably by mystical writers such as Lanspergio and Mallonius; by
theologians such as Gretser and Suarez; by historians such as Stengel
and Paleoti; by hagiographers and archaeologists such as Galesinus,
Gervais and Biondo. Calcaginus, quoted by Sandini and reproduced
by archdeacon Pamelius, gives his appreciation of the fact in the
following terms. "The effigy of Christ, which tradition states to have
been given to Veronica impressed upon the Sudarium, still exists, and
is held in so great veneration, that not only miracles, but even the
mere sight of the picture prevents any doubt from being entertained
in regard to it." Molanus strengthens this quotation by the opinion
of Alberic, who, in his dictionary of the year 1350, holds the same
language. "There is in the library of the Vatican, adds the Belgian
author, a history of the translation of the effigy in question to Rome,

under Tiberius, which is edited in a trustworthy manner, and of which the handwriting is very ancient in character. The celebrated English theologian, Thomas Stapleton, informed me that be bad read the whole of it. " Baronius confirms the existence of this precious manuscript, and he then says- "In the church of St. Mary of the Martyrs, there is preserved with the most jealous care, at the altar of the Crucifixion, the worm-eaten remains of a wooden coffer which was used for the transportation of the holy Relic. "Msgr. Barbier de Montaut, copied, in the above named church, the inscription which attests bow the holy Sudarium was brought in the hands of Veronica from Palestine to Rome. Struck by so general an agreement, the Bollandists formulated these two conclusions—"That the Sudarium was given to St. Veronica is accepted by orthodox Christians without hesitation. That Veronica herself conveyed the holy Picture to Rome is the unanimous opinion of all writers on the subject."

Let us here observe with Baronius that the veil used by Veronica and which she placed upon the face of the Christ covered with sweat and blood, must not be confounded with the most holy Sudarium, which is kept at Turin, and in which the adorable body of the Savior was enveloped and buried, or with the other linen cloths with which His Face and head where covered in the Holy Sepulcher.

The Latin word Sudarium signifies a handkerchief used for wiping away sweat. Such is the original meaning of the word, which Bergier thus defines in his *Theological Dictionary*— "A piece of linen or a handkerchief used for wiping the face." The action of Veronica is explained by the Jewish women being accustomed to wear on their heads or necks a woolen or linen veil, which they hastened to offer to persons of their acquaintance whom they might chance to see with their faces covered with sweat or bathed in tears.

In pagan times, it was also customary to present a veil to criminals condemned to death. This was done from a feeling of compassion, or as a sign of the interest taken in them. The veil was intended to dry their tears with and to cover their heads at the moment when they were about to be executed. We read in the life of St. Paul that as he was being led out of Rome, to be beheaded, and had arrived at the gate of the city, accompanied by a great crowd and in the midst of the people, he saw a lady, called Plautilla, who seemed to be very sorrowful and desolate; whereupon he asked of her a veil with which to make a bandage for his eyes (as was usual in the case of those who were to be beheaded), at the same time promising that it should be returned to her. She gave it to him willingly, and the apostle, on the following night, appeared lo her and restored her veil.

Veronica, therefore, did nothing more than conform with a custom which at that time was looked upon as usual; but is was nevertheless necessary for her to brave the fury of the soldiers and the insults of the maddened crowd. Therefore, she deserved that the Savior, touched by her devotion, should leave to her His holy Effigy as a sign of his eternal love. Her heroic action will be forever glorified throughout all ages; and pious souls will not cease lo bless her for the service and the honor rendered Lo Jesus in His sorrowful Passion.

It is said that Tiberius, after his cure, wished to heap favors and riches on his benefactress. But she refused all the offers of the Emperor, knowing well that she possessed a treasure compared with which everything besides was as nothing. She kept it with the utmost care and, afterwards, it became the inheritance and the treasure of the Church. All who testify to it, in act, are agreed in saying that she gave the "veil" to St. Clement, who was at that time the assistant and the coadjutor of St. Peter and who later on was his third successor.

Did St. Veronica die at Rome? Ferrari seems to say so. Pierre Galesinus gives her a place in his martyrology as having finished her days "in the very city to which she brought from Jerusalem the Face of the Lord." According to this opinion, it is thought that she was buried in the interior of the Vatican Basilica, not far from the august Picture itself. Nevertheless, neither her tomb nor her body is pointed out in a precise manner.

Did she die in Jerusalem? The revelation of Catherine Emmerich declare that she did, but even allowing these revelations, which after all possess but little historical value, to be true, still although the house of Veronica is shown at Jerusalem, no mention is anywhere made of her having been buried there.

Did she die in Gaul? It is so attested by a tradition, centuries old, belonging to the southern provinces of Gaul, and therefore worthy of attention for a moment. This tradition, it must be observed, rests upon the authority of the Dominican Bernard de la Guionie, Bishop of Lodeve. After having referred to the apostolic mission of St. Martial, in the year 47 of our era, the historian adds that "this same St. Martial, coming from Aquitaine, had with him a man of God, called Amateur, and his wife, whose name was Veronica. Amateur, cherishing a special predilection for solitude, remained for a long lime in the hollow of a rock which was afterwards known as Roc-Amadour. His body is there venerated. As to his wife Veronica, who faithfully followed the blessed Martial everywhere in bis preaching, and who listened to him with as much piety as devotedness, being at last overtaken by old age, she retired to the borders of the sea in the Bordelais territory. There the holy man of God, Martial, raised and consecrated, in honor of the blessed Virgin Mary, a chapel which bears the name of Soulac, because the milk of the Blessed Virgin was the only relic placed there, the other relics of the Blessed Virgin which Martial possessed having been distributed in various places."

This recital has been handed down to our own days as being the expression of a general belief. In 1485, Pope Martin V, declaring that the church of Roc-Amadour dates back to the foundation of Christianity, stales that St. Amateur was no other than Zacchaeus, the disciple of Christ, and that Veronica was his wife. In the seventeenth century the breviaries of Limoges, of Toulouse, of Bordeaux, of Cahors, of Carcassonne, of Tulle, of Agen, of Angonleme and of Periguenx, preserved the whole substance of the ancient legends relative to the facts which we have just related.

According to Father Bonaventure, who wrote in 1680, "St. Veronica died in the year 70, A. D. and was buried at Seurin. Nevertheless, on account of wars and other disturbances, her body was translated to Bordeaux and reposes in the church of St. Scurin." This translation took place about the ninth century, during the ravages of the Normans. For a long time, the feast of the Saint, occurring on the 4th of February, was celebrated at St. Seurin. The aspect of her body indicates great antiquity. One fragment is wanting; it is the femoral bone of the upper rib; the reason of it is known and is as follows. When an inventory was made of the relics of St. Seurin, on the 10th of October 1659, this fragment was given by the chapter of Bordeaux to the parish priest of St. Eustache at Paris, who had in his parish a celebrated confraternity established under the name of St. Veronica.

Not long ago, in February 1882, Cardinal Donnet, Archbishop of Bordeaux, wishing to give a relic to his friend Msgr. Bellot des Minieres, Bishop of Poitiers, ordered this ancient tomb to be opened. A commission of enquiry had been named, and a minute and careful examination was made of the bones. Their state enabled the great age of the subject to be verified, and it was calculated that, at the time of the Passion and when she received the ineffable impression of the features of the Savior, Veronica must have been about 50 years old. At the age of 64 or 65 she must have gone with the mission to Gaul, where she died on the shores of Notre-Dame de la Fin-des-Terres, at about the age of 87.

Such is the tradition followed by the Churches of Aquitaine. It has been ably sustained to the present day in several remarkable works[4]. Nevertheless, between Rome, which asserts that Veronica died within her walls, and Bordeaux, which claims her body, we cannot pronounce any certain decision. The question, moreover, belongs only indirectly to our subject, and it suffices us to know that, according to the testimony given by the whole body of authors, the veil of Veronica remains in the eternal City. It is at Home consequently that we may fix our starting point in order thence to follow the successive phases of the cultus rendered to the precious Effigy.

II

Pope St. Clement, the third successor of St. Peter, ruled over the Church from the year 93 lo 402, A. D. The sacred Relic which Veronica desired should be given into his care, was transmitted by him to his successors who, during the era of the persecutions of the Church, kept it with the greatest secrecy[5].

---

4. Amongst others by Msgr. Cirot de la Ville, in his beautiful work on the Origines chretieunes de Bordeaux.

5. The following pages are almost entirely taken from the learned Italian Dictionary of Moroni. We have adhered faithfully to the translation made by M. d'Avrainville, the intimate friend or M. Dupont, his pious widow having recently consented to place his precious manuscript in our bands.

With regard to specifying in what place, after peace back been secured to the Church the Relic was at first placed, writers on the subject have not arrived at any agreement. Some think that it was deposited in the basilica of the Vatican, after it had been constructed by Constantine the Great, and consecrated by Pope St. Sylvester. Others indicate the church of St. Mary of the Martyrs, the ancient Pantheon of Agrippa, as being a place well fortified and therefore very secure, seeing that it was situated almost in the center of the inhabited portion of Rome, and at the same time was vast enough to receive the crowds of people who resorted there on certain days to honor the effigy of the Savior, whilst on the other hand the basilica of St. Peter, which for a long time was outside the walls, did not offer the same security. Those who hold the latter opinion also affirm that the Holy Face was venerated. at St. Mary of the Martyrs as early as the year 610, A. D., and during the reign of Boniface IV, who officiated at the dedication of the celebrated temple. They state that it began to be exposed solemnly at that time on the high altar on the 13th of May, the anniversary of the memorable dedication, in 608, A. D., on which day the Sovereign Pontiff translated thither, upon twenty-eight funeral carts, the bodies of holy martyrs which had been taken from the catacombs.

There is still preserved, in the above named church, the remains of the coffer or reliquary in which the sacred Picture was enclosed. We have already referred to what Baronius has said respecting it. A careful examination of the remains of this coffer shows that formerly ten locks were attached to it. The keys were confided to the ten ancient Rioni, or quarters of Rome, in such a manner that the holy Relic was placed under the care of the whole city, and the reliquary could not be opened, except in presence of its representatives.

These precious remains are now enclosed in an urn and placed under a glass upon the table of the altar of the Crucifix, in a hollow of the wall; and on it is the following inscription— "The coffer in which the sacred Sudarium was taken from Palestine to Rome by St. Veronica. It shed luster on this basilica during one hundred years."

It appears that St. Veronica, the better to preserve the Holy Face, enclosed it in two coffers or reliquaries, one of which is that of which we have just spoken. The other is venerated in the church of Saint-Eloi-des-Serruriers. Piazza Vasi, in his Itinerary, and several other authors think that this latter was the inner reliquary or coffer.

As to the preservation and the veneration of the Holy Face in the Vatican Basilica, the most trustworthy writers on the subject, and the most competent authorities prove that John VII in the year 707, A. D., having constructed for "the Blessed Virgin of the Crib" an oratory which he desired should also be the place of his sepulcher, raised an altar there in honor of "the Holy Sudarium of Jesus Christ, called the Veronica," and placed the Holy Face in a large and beautiful tabernacle ornamented with marble pillars; the chapel itself also received the same title and was known as "St. Mary of the Su*darium*," as is evident from a document of the year 1017, A. D., in which John VII is styled *clerk and chaplain of St. Mary of the Veronica.* Torrigio, in his *Holy Vatican Grottoes,* speaking of the tabernacle, which contains the effigy of our Lord, is not afraid of calling it "the Holy of Holies". The same historian also says that under Adrian VI "double locks were affixed to the tabernacle." It was, moreover, surrounded by a balcony from which the Holy Face was displayed in sight of the people. Mabillon speaks of a Roman Ceremonial Book of the year 1130, A. D., in which it is said- "Then the Pontiff goes to the *Sudarium* of Christ,

called the Veronica, and incenses it[6]." Alveri affirms, together with
other authors, that, in the time of Pope Innocent II, six noble Roman
families were appointed as guards of the Holy Face and had under
their charge the reliquary in which it was enclosed. In his "History
of remarkable Objects belonging to the Vatican Basilica," dedicated to
Alexander II, 1159, A. D., Mallio attests the special veneration which
the Holy Face enjoyed at that epoch; ten lamps being kept burning
before it day and night[7].

Medals also existed and were called "Veronicas." They bore the
effigy of the Holy Face with the crossed keys of St. Peter on the obverse
side; pilgrims, full of confidence in these pious objects, attached them
to their hats and to their coats. So great was the veneration professed
for the august Effigy, that it was often represented on Pontifical coins,
which on that account were styled— *Signum Veronicae*[8]. Scilla, in
his work on *Pontifical Coins,* gives several specimens of them stamped
with the effigy of the Holy Face.

Cancellieri, in his *Memoirs respecting* the *Heads of the Holy Apostles*
Peter *and Paul,* relates that, in 1193, Philip Augustus, King of France,
having come to Rome, Pope Celestine III ordered them to he shown
to him together with "the Veronica, that is to say the piece of linen
which Jesus Christ applied to His Face, and which has so marvelously
preserved the impression of it down to the present day, that it might
be believed to be the very Face itself of the Savior. It is called Veronica,

---

6. Postea vadit Pontifex ad Sudarium Christi, quod vocatur
   Veronica, et incensat.

7. Ante Veronicam decem lampadae die nocteque.

8. Signum Veronicae

the writer observes, from the name of the woman to whom the linen belonged, and whose name was Veronica"[9]. Pope Innocent III, who occupied the Holy See in 1198, A. D., had a great veneration for the Holy Face; he composed prayers in its honor; prescribing that they should be recited before the august Face, and he also attached Indulgences to their recital. Matthew of Westminster attributes to the same Pape the following incident-. "He had the Holy Face, called the Veronica, carried in a solemn procession, that the people might see it. On his return from the ceremony, it was put back in its place, but on the following day it was found thrown down, with the face towards the ground. Fearing that this accident was an omen of evil, the Holy Father composed a collect in honor of the Holy Face, and granted an indulgence of ten days to those who should recite it[10]."

Cancellieri[11] relates, without definitely stating the date, that the Holy Face was transferred to the hospital of the Holy Ghost, and he

---

9. Cancellieri : *Veronicam, id est pannum quemdam lineum quem Jesus Christus vultui suo impressit, in quo pressura illa ita manifeste usque in hodiernum diem apparet, ac si vultus Jesu Christi ibi esset, et dicitur Veronica, quia mulier,* cujus pannus ille erat, Veronica dicebatur.

10. Sainte Veronica, apotre de l'Aquitaine, p. 256. This collect is perhaps the prayer which the Bollandistes mention,without quoting it, and to which Innocent II granted forty days of indulgences. They state that it is to be found in the Missal of Augsburg of 1555, and in the Missal of Mayence, printed in 1693.

11. Settimana Santa, p. 146.

quotes an ancient chronicle according to which the holy Picture was placed in a small chamber, entirely constructed of marble and iron, and locked with six keys which were confided to six Roman families. It was shown only once a year, and six gentlemen, who had the honor of keeping the keys, enjoyed all the franchises of the city and were exempt from active military service. If to any one of them it foll by lot to be seneschal, that is to say to assist the judges at the tribunal, he was not obliged to be present. Whenever the "ostension" (or the exposition of the Holy Relics) took place it was their duty , each one of them being accompanied by twenty chosen men at arms, to surround the Holy Relic, to accompany it to the place designated and to replace it in its chamber under lock and key. It was probably on account of, and in memory of the temporary sojourn of the Holy Face at the hospital, that Innocent III. instituted, by a bull of 1208, A. D., a procession which it was customary to make every year on the first Sunday after the octave of the Epiphany, and in which the Holy Face was carried solemnly from the Vatican Basilica to the church of the Holy Ghost, accompanied by the Cardinals and in the presence of the Sovereign Pontiff, who addressed a sermon to the people. On this occasion an alms of three denarii was given to a thousand poor foreigners and to three hundred of the said hospital. The Holy Relic remained sometime in the church of the Holy Ghost and was afterwards taken back to the Vatican Basilica.

A trace of these customs is to be found in one of the homilies pronounced on that day by Innocent III. The Pope, when alluding to the marriage feast of Cana recalled to mind by the Gospel of the Sunday, said- "We also invite to this marriage feast the Son of Mary, Jesus Christ, with His disciples, seeing that His priests are today bringing here with great veneration His Holy Face in order that the faithful people, hastening hither impelled by piety and to implore mercy, may contemplate and admire its glory according to their ardent desire. Let not one of them retire from this wedding feast without being satisfied. All who have come hither to celebrate with promptitude and gladness this solemnity will receive the indulgence of one year, and the divine Spouse, Jesus Christ, who is blessed for ever and ever, will thereby change water into wine."

Honorius III, the successor of Innocent III, mentions this procession with the privileges attached to it in a letter addressed to the Brothers of the Hospital, in 1224— "As Jesus, he says, was invited with His disciples to the wedding of Cana, where His Mother also went, we it right to decree, since this hospital is under the protection of the most Blessed Virgin, that the Canons of St. Peter's should convey hither the Holy Face of Jesus Christ, in its reliquary of gold and silver, enriched with precious stones, in order to show it to the faithful who may resort here in crowds for the purpose of venerating it. And in order that we who exhibit and enable others to venerate this sacred treasure, should give to our neighbor an example worthy of imitation, we grant, decree and order that alms should be distributed to a thousand poor people outside the walls of the hospital and to three hundred poor within it. This alms must consist of seventeen livres of current coin, of which sum each person will receive three denarii: one for bread, one for wine, and one for meat. These alms will be paid to you every year in perpetuity by the almoner of the Sovereign Pontiff. In addition, each of the Canons who shall have borne the Holy Face in procession shall receive twelve ecus and a taper weighing one pound, which he shall carry lighted. The expenses will be defrayed out of the oblations of the Confession of St. Peter. And as man does not live by bread alone, but by every word which proceeds out of the mouth of God, the Sovereign Pontiff shall assist at this procession with the Cardinals, shall celebrate the Mass and shall address an exhortation to the pilgrims on the subject of the solemnity. Moreover, that the faithful people may not have to return fasting from this sacred marriage feast, they shall receive an indulgence of one year for the remission of the temporal punishment due to their sins[12]."

The other Popes of the thirteenth century confirmed these privileges. Later on, about 1474, Sixtus IV, actuated by just motives, abolished the procession and substituted for it another which proceeds every year, on the same day, to venerate the Holy Face in the Basilica itself. The members of the Archconfraternity of "Santo Pietro in Sassia," which already existed in 1198 and which for some time enjoyed the honor of watching over the august Relic, doubtless succeeded to the six gentlemen of Rome. At the present day they betake themselves processionally to St. Peter's on the first Sunday after the octave of the Epiphany, as well as on Whit-Monday; and the Holy Face is exhibited to them by privilege. Three times a year it is also shown, by special privilege, to the foundlings of both sexes and to the ecclesiastics of the hospital of the Holy Ghost, in remembrance of the sojourn that the august Relic made there in former days.

When Boniface VIII reestablished, in 1300, the celebration of the "holy year", he permitted the Holy Face to be shown every Friday and on all solemn feasts in the Vatican Basilica, for the consolation of pilgrims who resorted in great numbers to Rome from all parts of the world in order to gain the Jubilee Indulgence. The same Pope made the "ostension" of it to Charles II, King of Sicily, and to James II, King of Aragon.

In 1350, Clement VI, although sojourning in Avignon, caused the second universal Jubilee to be celebrated at Rome. The concourse of

---

12. Sainte Veronica, p. 260.

pilgrims to the city, on this occasion, was immense. The Pope wrote to the Canons of the Vatican in order to recommend lo them the frequent "ostension" of the Holy Face, because of the great devotion of the faithful towards so precious a relic. Louis I, King of Hungary, solicited and obtained from the same Pontiff the favor of venerating it everyday.

Generally speaking, it appeared that the Sovereign Pontiffs were glad to permit the "ostensions" of the veil of St. Veronica, and to institute feasts and periodical processions in its honor. Pope Sixtus IV, in a bull concerning the election of two benefices, declares that the Vatican Basilica surpasses all the other churches of Rome and of the universe, because of its possession of the "Holy Sudarium" of our Lord, by which he means the effigy of the Holy Face. Nicholas IV, in the year 1290, observes that it is "in the said Basilica that the Lord willed that the precious impression of His Holy Face, known by the name of Veronica, should be deposited, together with the body of St. Peter and those of a great number of Saints."

Several other Popes, such as Celestine II, Clement VII, Clement VIII, and Gregory XIII, mention the relic of the Holy Face, attest to a devotion to it which never ceases to increase, and always take for granted the existence of the heroic woman to whom the Savior gave this special testimony of his love.

Benedict XIV brings to bear upon this subject his undoubted authority in matters of science and criticism- "In the Basilica of the Vatican," he says, "in addition to the spear and the lance, is preserved and greatly venerated the Sudarium which has perfectly kept and still keeps the impression of the face of our Lord Jesus Christ, bathed with sweat and blood."

More than once, in the midst of the wars and bloody revolutions of which Rome was too often the theatre, the Holy Face was translated to and placed in safety in the castle of St. Angelo. Thus, according to a journal of that date, Cancellieri relates that on "the 4th of October of the year 1410, the Sudarium of St. Veronica was taken from the sacristy of St. Peter's to the castle of St. Angelo, that it might not be exposed to the insults of the soldiers."

In 1450, Pope Nicholas V had three small bells cast which gave forth a silvery and harmonious sound. They were used to announce the "ostension" of the Holy Relic, as is still done at the present day. On each of the bells are the armorial bearings of the Pontiff, with these words engraved around them- "Pope Nicholas V made me in the year of the Jubilee 1450." The same Pope, in 1452, after having crowned Frederic III Emperor, and created him Canon of the Vatican, as was the custom, granted to him the special favor of being able , in canonical costume, to ascend to the tabernacle of the Holy Face, there to venerate the august Relic, and to show it to the people- a favor which was not and up to the present time has never been granted except to the Canons of the Basilica.

When Pope Innocent VIII, in 1492, received as a gift from the Emperor of Turks the Holy Lance which pierced the side of the Redeemer, he preserved it in his own chamber, proposing to himself to construct a sumptuous chapel for it in the basilica of St. Peter; but finding that his end was approaching, the Pontiff ordered that the precious Relic should be placed in the chapel of the "most Holy Sudarium."

It was Pope Urban VIII who had the Holy Face deposited in the place which he had destined for it, under the great dome, the masterpiece of Michael Angelo, in the recently constructed Basilica of St. Peter. The ceremony took place on the 23rd of December of the holy year 1625. The Holy Face and the holy Lance, which had been temporarily deposited in the archives of the Basilica and enclosed in an iron coffer covered with a piece of rich damask, were carried in procession and under a canopy to the great niche known as that of "St. Veronica." The canopy was carried by the Archduke Leopold, son of the Emperor Ferdinand III, and by other illustrious personages.

In order further to increase the veneration of the faithful towards the holy Effigy, Urban VIII decreed that on the 8th of April 1629, there should be added to the Holy Face and holy Lance a piece of the wood of the true Cross; he also ordained by a bull that the three august Relics should always be shown one after the other, granting a plenary Indulgence to all who should be present at the "ostension". The Sovereign Pontiff himself went there at two o'clock in the afternoon, and, prostrating himself before the three holy Holies, he venerated them with great devotion; and under pain of excommunication, he forbade, by a proclamation which was affixed to the niche, that the gauze veil which covered the Holy Face should be removed without a papal authorization. The same Pope, Urban VIII, conferred upon Wladislaus, son of Sigismund III, King of Poland, on the occasion of his making him a visit, the mantle and blessed sword in recompense for his courageous devotion to the Church. Then, by a special favor, he created him Canon of St. Peter's, so that he might, in that quality, be enabled to venerate, near at band, the Holy Face. The prince, clad in a surplice and rochet, ascended to the tabernacle where the sacred Effigy was kept, and was authorized to show "it solemnly to the people, with the assistance of the other Canons. Seven years afterwards, having become King of Poland under the name of Wladislaus VII, he received from the Chapter and the Canons of St. Peter's a letter of congratulation to which he made the following gracious answer-- "We have not forgotten that during our sojourn at Rome we were aggregated to your sacred College, in order that we might be permitted to contemplate the most Holy Face of our Lord."

Como, Grand Duke of Tuscany, came to Rome, in 1700, to gain the Indulgences of the Jubilee and to venerate the holy Effigy. Pope Innocent XII also made him a Canon, that he might hold the precious Relic in his hands. He ascended to the loggia clad in a violet soutane, rochet, baretta and reel gloves, according to the custom still observed amongst ourselves, and after having piously venerated the divine picture, he made the "ostension" of it to the people, and blessed them with it, standing between two Canons. A picture at the Vatican represents him in canonical costume.

At an epoch nearer to our own, Pope Pius VII permitted the King of Sardinia, Emmanuel IV and the Queen his wife, the venerable Marie-Clotilde of France, to contemplate and kiss the Holy Face of our Lord, in the vestibule of the oratory where it is kept. A similar favor was granted by the same Pope, in 1801, to the pious Archduchess Marie-Anne of Austria, who had just received the holy Eucharist in the Basilica. When she had satisfied her devotion, the Canons standing in the loggia above, blessed the persons of her suite and all the faithful present with the precious Relic.

On Easter Monday 1806, after the papal chapel, the same sovereign Pontiff, Pius VII, went to the Vatican Basilica with his noble guard; then preceded by lighted torches and assisted by two Canons, he ascended to the shrine of the Veronica. There, after having prayed for some time before the three holy Relics, he permitted all the persons of his suite to approach and venerate at their ease the glorious memorials of our redemption.

We now arrive at the memorable epoch of the reign of Pius IX. Towards the fourth year of his Pontificate, God deigned to glorify, by a touching prodigy, the Effigy venerated at the Vatican. It was during the exile of the Holy Father at Gaeta, in 1849, and at the period when the Holy Face is permitted to be publicly exposed, from Christmas to the Epiphany. Now, the third day of the exposition, the veil of Veronica became suddenly suffused with color and the Face of our Lord appeared as though animated with life in the midst of a soft light. On this occasion the divine Face appeared distinctly upon the veil, the impression on which is very slight, appearing the more so on account of it being seen through a plate of crystal which covers it, and prevents the features from being clearly visible. But, at that moment, it appeared in relief and of a cadaverous color, the eyes sunken and wearing an expression of profound severity. The Canons who were keeping guard near the holy Relic immediately caused their colleagues to be informed, as well as all the clergy of the Basilica; the two great bells were rung and the people hastened to the church. The faces of all wore an indescribable expression, many wept and all were struck with awe by the miracle. An apostolic notary was summoned and an act drawn up, affirming the fact. This astonishing miracle lasted three hours. The same evening some veils of white silk on which bad been engraved the effigy of the Holy Face were touched with it and sent to France[13].

It was in consequence of this event, in the midst of the sorrowful trials of the Church, that the custom was introduced into France of asking for authentic copies of the veil of Veronica to be sent from Rome, and of showing them special devotion..

In 1854, when the dogma of the Immaculate Conception of Mary was defined, the Cardinal Vicar in an "Invito Sagro," announced to the city of Rome that, by order of the Holy Father, the three major Relics would be exposed upon an altar of the Vatican Basilica from the first Sunday in Advent being the 3rd of December, till the following

---

13. Vie de M. Dupont, v. II, ch. 1, p. 10.

Thursday at noon. The Holy Face and the two other precious Relics were placed on the altar of the Blessed Sacrament, below the canopy, in order that the greatest possible number or the Bishops who had come to Rome for the event might have the consolation or celebrating the august Sacrifice before the holy Relics. It was the first time that the Holy Face was exposed for so many days upon an altar in the Basilica of St Peter; the Sovereign Pontiff desiring by means of this special favor to enhance the glorious promulgation of the most beautiful privilege of the Blessed Virgin, a promulgation which had been waited for during eighteen centuries, and which was calculated to excite immense gladness in heaven and on earth.

III

It is thus that the celebrated Relic, the history of which we have been tracing, has been preserved to the present day. From the time of the third successor of St. Peter, Pope St. Clement, to whom it was delivered, down to that of Leo XIII, now reigning, the divine Effigy has never ceased to be carefully preserved by the Sovereign Pontiff's; they have all of them watched over it with pious care, and have all of them been inspired with respect and with love for it.

At their voice, the faithful have always hastened to venerate it from all parts of the universe. During the different Jubilees and on the privileged days when the venerable Face was exposed, crowds filled the church of St. Peter overflowing, chanting liturgical canticles and intoning the prayer- "Hail, Holy Face of our Redeemer, wherein is reflected, as in a clear mirror, the splendor of our God. Impressed upon a veil white as snow, Thou wast given to Veronica as a token of love. Hail, ornament of the world, mirror of Saints. Purify us, Thou whom the heavenly host desire to contemplate; cleanse us from every stain and unite us to the company of the Blessed."

The pilgrims, after having adored the Holy Face, took away
with them copies of it. Towards 1333, the Prince Royal of Vienna,
Humbert II, made a provision of them, as well as of many other
objects which he purchased whilst visiting the churches of Rome. In
the sixteenth century, Jean de Dumex was the official painter at the
court of Rome who was charged with the duty of distributing these
"Veronicas" throughout the Christian world. In the time of Innocent
III, medals representing the Holy Face were struck, and those who sold
them were called "Veronica merchants."

St. Bridget reproaches, in the name of Jesus Christ, several of her
contemporaries, because of the doubts they had expressed respecting
the effigy of the Holy Face. Dante, in his immortal poem, re-echoing
the belief of his epoch, meets Veronica in Paradise, holding her
veil, and he exclaims with admiration- "Oh my Lord Jesus Christ,
true God! it is thus then that Thy Holy Face has been preserved!"
John Dorat, another poet, celebrates it as the most admirable of all
paintings, because it was traced upon the veil of Veronica, not by the
hand of man, but by the face of God Himself.

During a long period, it was forbidden, under pain of
excommunication, to reproduce copies of the holy Effigy, and we are
cognizant of only two authentic replicas made of it in past centuries;
that namely of Montreuil-sous-Laon, which will form the subject of
a special notice, and that granted by Gregory XV, in 1621, to a lady of
the Sforza family, who made a gift of it to the House of the Society of
Jesus at Rome, where it is still venerated in the chapel known as "the
Chamber of St. Ignatius."

The Sovereign Pontiffs have of late years, departed from their
former strictness. They have authorized copies of the holy Effigy,
printed upon linen, cotton or silk, to be made; they are then
impressed with a seal and furnished with a guarantee; these faithful

reproductions are permitted to he exposed in different parts of the Catholic world, in order to reanimate faith and true piety in the hearts of the people.

The "ostensions" of the Holy Face in the Vatican Basilica, are also made more frequently now than in former days. They take place as follows-

On the first Sunday after the octave of the Epiphany, and on Whit-Monday, for the associates of the Archconfraternity of the Holy Ghost;

On Wednesday in Holy Week, after the Tenebrae;

On Holy Thursday and Good Friday, several times during the day;

On Holy Saturday, after mass;

On Easter Sunday, after the papal mass, for the Pope, the Cardinals and all such persons as have taken part in the ceremony;

On Easter Monday, before and after vespers;

On Ascension Day, after mass;

On the 3rd of May, the feast of the Invention of the holy Cross;

On the 18th of November, the anniversary of the dedication of the Basilica;

On the 18th of January, the feast of the Chair of St. Peter at Rome;·

On the 22nd of February, the feast of the Chair of St. Peter at Antioch;

Lastly, in calamities of the Church, or of the Holy See; in case of war, of earthquake, of pestilence, or of the inundation of the Tiber; on extraordinary Jubilees, or in penitential processions.

The three precious Relics, called the "Major Relics," are kept at the present day in a niche or oratory situated in the interior of one of the four pentagonal pillars which support the great dome of St. Peter's, on the epistle side of the papal altar.

The shrine which contains them is ornamented exteriorly with a bas-relief representing the Holy Face. Below it, placed on the basement, is the marble statue of St. Veronica, fifteen fect high, holding the Holy Face in her bands; it is due to the chisel of Mochi, an Italian sculptor of the seventeenth century. It occupies one of the lower niches, made in the great pillars which sustain the dome; an honor which it shares with St. Helena, whose statue bears a great cross, with St. Longinus, who holds a lance, and with the apostle St. Andrew, brother of St. Peter. A door, situated at the foot of the statue of St. Veronica, gives access to two passages, one of which leads to the niche above, where the holy Relies arc deposited, and the other, after descending a few steps, to what are called "the Vatican Grottoes;" the name by which the subterranean space is called which is the nearest to the ancient cemetery or "Vatican Arenaire," between the pavement of the present and a portion of the ancient basilica. In these holy grottoes repose the body of St. Peter and the tombs of a great number of Popes whose monuments are placed in the modem basilica. There also are the four subterranean chapels which, by order of Urban VIII, Bernini constructed in the interior of the pillars supporting the great cupola. He decorated them with Ionic columns of breccia, and placed above the altars very precious mosaic pictures.

We shall now describe the altar of the Holy Face.

The picture over it represents Veronica offering her veil to the Redeemer. On the walls are depicted the Blessed Virgin and the three Maries. On the first oval of the vault, Pope Urban VIII receives from the architect Bernini the plan of the four chapels; on the second, Pope Boniface VIII shows the Holy Face to Charles II, King of Sicily, and to James, King of Aragon; the third recalls to mind the "ostcusion" made by order of Pope Nicholas V to the Emperor Frederic III.

On the gospel side of the walls of the corridor Veronica is seen presenting her veil to the Savior, on either side are the sisters Mary and Martha, whilst, opposite to them Veronica is seen making ready to leave Rome with the Holy Sudarium; Mary mother of James and Maria Salome are also represented, together with the Virgin Mary and Mary mother of Cleophas.

The paintings on the vault recall to remembrance the following facts- Veronica showing the holy Sudarium to the people, John VII presenting the tabernacle raised by his piety for the preservation of the precious Relic[14], and lastly the Holy Face shown to Louis I, King of Hungary, by order of Pope Clement VI.

If, instead of descending to the grottoes, we wish to reach the niche whence the "ostension" is made, we open an iron door placed at the left, and passing through it we arrive, by means of a spiral staircase, at the sanctuary of the holy Relics. They repose on a credence table, itself enclosed in a niche secured by three locks, the keys of which are confided to the Sacristan Canons in chief, who have the charge of these precious treasures. The Holy Face is placed in a separate reliquary of magnificent crystal adorned with plates of silver, offered on the 6th of May of the Jubilee year 1350 by three Venetian nobles, whose names are preserved in a very ancient register of the benefactors of the Basilica.

By a singular coincidence, in 1838, it was another illustrious Venetian, the Sovereign Pontiff Gregory XVI, who took the wise precaution of substituting, for the thin veil which covered the Holy

---

14. In the chapel which the Pope constructed in honor of the "Virgin of the crib."

Face, a plate of crystal, behind which it is better preserved and venerated.

The aspect of the august Face is of itself alone sufficient to show the accuracy of its resemblance to the divine Face of our Lord, even if the innumerable miracles which it has worked, and the veneration of which it has been the object in all ages did not attest the truth of the catholic tradition. The Christ has left upon it the impress of His majestic and venerable Effigy in the lamentable state to which it was reduced when he was ascending the Mount of Calvary. Its aspect is that of overwhelming grief and so affecting is its expression that it is impossible to look at it without experiencing a profound emotion which penetrates the inmost heart with reverence and compunction[15] .

Piazza, who wrote at the beginning of the last century (1713), after having recounted the history of St. Veronica in his Calendrier de Rome, on the 4th of February, gives the following description of

---

15. Effigies Christi, quam Veronicae in sudario dedisse traditio est, etiam nunc exstat tanta in veneratione, ut illa dubitare posthac non modo miracula non permittant, sed nec aspect us ipse, "the portrait of Jesus Christ, which tradition states to have been given to Veronica upon her Sudarium, is now the object of such great veneration that not only miracles but even the mere view of the Sudarium does not allow any doubt to be entertained of the fact." (Pamelius, in his annotations upon the twelfth chapter of Tertullian's Apology.)

the Holy Face, which description is confirmed by other trustworthy authors[16] --

"The head of the Christ, he says, is everywhere transpierced with thorns; the forehead is bleeding, the eyes swollen and bloodshot, the face pale and livid. Upon the right cheek the cruel mark of the blow given by Malchus[17] with his iron gauntlet sorrowfully attracts observation, in the same manner as do the spittle of the Jews and the stains left upon the left cheek. The nose is a little flattened and bleeding, the mouth open and filled with blood; the beard torn out in several places and the hair also on one side. Thus disfigured, the Holy Face, nevertheless, presents to us in its whole aspect a blending of majesty and of compassion, of love and of sadness, which at the great solemnities, when it is shown in the Vatican Basilica to the immense concourse of people attracted thither by the splendor of the ceremonial, causes this most holy Picture a living testimony, as it is, of the ingratitude of man, to inspire a salutary fear in the breasts of all who look upon it, whilst it also gives birth to a confidence mingled with sorrow and sincere repentance in the hearts of the faithful in whom it awakes, by abundant tears of penitence, an ardent love for our most sweet Redeemer."

This description of the historian exactly corresponds with the copies of the veil of Veronica as they are sent from Rome, with the

---

16. Especially Gio Gregorio in his book Du Pretoire de Pilate (liv. XVII).

17. John Lanspergius, homily 10, De Passione, writes- Quod Christi Facies in eodem impressa sudario digitorurn vestigia retineat, et aspicientibus monstrat, quod armata manu Christo Domino inflixere.

seal, the certificate and the signature of a Canon of the Vatican Basilica impressed upon them. Whatever may be the opinion pronounced upon these engravings as works of art, they produce upon the attentive beholder an impression which is quite indescribable[18] , and he is ready to exclaim with the Psalmist- "I have entreated Thy Face with my whole heart, have pity on me according to Thy promise" (Psalm cxxiii, 58). "Let the light of Thy countenance shine upon me, and save me in Thy mercy" (Psalm xxx, 15). In common with a certain great servant of God, M. Dupont, who died at Tours in the odor of sanctity, on the 18th of March 1876, he will also love to repeat those words of St. Edme, Archbishop of Canterbury- "May I expire panting with an ardent thirst to see the desirable Face of Jesus Christ!"

Having now reached the conclusion of this notice, we will give a short summary of what we have said respecting the Holy Face of the Vatican.

It is certain that our Lord Jesus Christ deigned to give us an effigy of Himself, and to leave to a holy woman called Veronica the miraculous impression of His Holy Face upon her veil.

It is certain that the moment chosen, in preference by Him, for representing Himself on the veil of His servant was that in which, bearing his cross and ascending the path which led to Calvary; He was about to accomplish the great work of the redemption of the human race.

---

18. This is especially the case with regard to the authentic copy which was received by M. Dupont in 1851 , and which he venerated with such great faith during twenty-five years of his life. The city or Tours has now the happiness of possessing it at the Oratory of the Holy Face.

It is certain that He willed to reproduce upon the veil of Veronica the features of His Holy Face, under a sorrowful aspect, such as it then bore, disfigured and worn, wounded and bleeding, covered with spittle and stains.

It is certain that He made use of Veronica herself to take her miraculous veil direct to Rome, and to place it in the hands of the third successor of St. Peter.

It is certain that He has constantly taken care that, in the midst of persecutions, disasters and wars of all kinds, the holy Effigy should be preserved and kept intact down to the present day, and that it should still be an object of public veneration, and or the most solemn homage.

It is certain that all the Sovereign Pontiffs, from century to century, guarded it with the most jealous care and that they finally deposited it in a place of honor near the tomb of the Holy Apostles, under the great dome of the Vatican Basilica, and in a special oratory, where, on certain days, it is exposed between the holy Lance and the true Cross.

Lastly, it is certain that in these latter days, it is easy to obtain the favor, formerly very rare, of obtaining authentic copies, from Rome, for the purpose of having them conveyed to and venerated in all the different parts of the world.

In presence of these providential facts, so wonderfully linked together, it is impossible not to see in them the express design of our Lord Jesus Christ, that His sorrowful Face should be the object of a special devotion in the Catholic Church. Does it not seem as though He were showing us in the veil of Veronica, and in the copies which reproduce it, a sign of salvation, a means of reparation, a symbol of mercy expressly reserved for the present generation to help it to become reconciled with the Divine Majesty, outraged as it is by so many crimes and blasphemies.

Oh you, who seek the most efficacious means of saving yourselves, and of saving those who are dear to you, turn your minds and hearts to the city of the Popes! Receive from her the warrant of deliverance and pardon. Render homage to the faithful and touching copy of the venerable Effigy of which she is the guardian. Look on the divine Face of your Savior, weeping, suffering, expiring through grief and love of you! At the sight of it let your hard hearts be softened and touched with compassion. Present it to the heavenly Father, saying with the accents of faith and the humility of a contrite heart- "Oh God, our Protector, behold the state to which we are reduced, look at the Face of Thy Christ, and save us."

THE HOLY FACE OF MONTREUIL-SOUS-LAON

We have already stated that, amongst the rare copies of the Holy Face of the Vatican approved in past centuries by the Sovereign Pontiffs, one of the most celebrated is that which is honored at the present day at Notre-Dame de Laon. We will endeavor briefly to sketch the history of it[1].

On the confines of Thierache and of Hainault, there flourished at Montreuil-Les-Dames in the thirteenth century, a Convent of Benedictine Nuns. They owed their foundation to Bartholomew de Vir, Bishop of Laon, and had received their rule from the great Abbot

---

1.

of Clairvaux, St. Bernard. These fervent Nuns added to prayers, fasting and many mortifications, the labor of their hands by tilling the ground with spade and hatchet. They cultivated in this way the land in their own neighborhood, cut clown forests, and gave to the soil the fertility it still enjoys. Historians and chroniclers of the time praise their austerity and their virtues. They had a special love for holy relics and religious pictures, which they sought eagerly and earnestly as furnishing them with subjects of contemplation and a means of increasing their fervor. We find, for example, that, at the beginning of the thirteenth century, they possessed a piece of the true Cross, which one of their abbesses enclosed in a silver cross richly chased.

Their devotion asked for yet more than this, and, knowing the veneration which the Holy Face of our Lord impressed upon the veil of Veronica enjoyed at Rome, they cherished a lively desire to possess a faithful copy of it. This pious longing was fed in their hearts by the sight of medals which bore on them an effigy of the Holy Face, and which, at that time, pilgrims were wont to bring from Rome. At last, circumstances, arranged by Providence, permitted them to have their devotion satisfied beyond their utmost hopes.

Towards the year 1249, Montreuil had for its Abbess a Nun called Sybil, whose brother resided at Rome and later on was elected Sovereign Pontiff. He was no other than Pope Urban IV, known before his elevation by the name of Jacques Pantaleon, or Jacques de Troyes, for he was of French origin, and a native of Troyes in Champagne. His parentage was rather obscure; at first a choir boy in the Cathedral of Laon, he pursued a course of studies in the school of the chapter, studies which were accompanied with such success, that he became not only a celebrated lawyer, but a learned theologian, and, in the end, was nominated to the post of chaplain to Pope Innocent III, and to that of treasurer of St. Peter's of the Vatican.

Sybil, his sister, was herself a woman of rare merit and of great virtue. The Nuns at Montreuil, profiting by the opportunity, begged their abbess to request her brother to obtain for them a copy of the famous veil of Veronica, the care of which was confided to him in his character of treasurer of the Vatican Basilica, "in order," they said, "to encourage themselves, by the contemplation of this divine object, to make further progress in the crucified life which they had embraced." Jacques Pantaleon, after having made many urgent representations to the Sovereign Pontiff, who placed all kinds of difficulties in the way of granting his request, at last obtained permission to have a copy of the celebrated picture made. When granting this permission, the Pope added that he himself intended to be present whilst the copy was being taken, perhaps to give more importance to the undertaking by his presence, or from a presentiment of the miracle that our Lord was about to work in favor of his dear spouses, the Nuns of Montreuil.

Now, according to a pious legend, which has become popular and has been related by historians, "the day which the Pope had fixed to have this copy made having arrived, His Holiness, accompanied by his chaplain and the officers of his court, betook himself to the church of St. Peter of the Vatican. The holy Veronica was then taken down in his presence from the elevated position where it was usually exposed, and the painter whom the Pope had selected was invited to approach it. But whilst he was attentively considering the divine Effigy, before making the first sketch of it with his pencil, he fell suddenly backwards and was seized with a kind of fainting fit, which greatly surprised the persons who where present at the spectacle. They were much more astonished, however, when the artist, having come to himself and proceeding to begin his work, they perceived that an invisible hand had painted upon the panel, during his fainting fit, an effigy which resembled the Veronica so closely, that it might have been taken for the holy veil itself[2]."

Jacques Pantaleon received this miraculous Effigy, and, with the approbation of the Pope, sent it with all due care to Montreuil, adding to it a letter for the Abbess and the Nims, the original of which was preserved until the revolution, in the archives of the monastery.

We make from this curious document the following extracts--

"To our venerable and pious sisters, cherished in the Lord, the Abbess and Nuns of the Convent at Montreuil, Jacques of Troyes, Archdeacon of Laon, Chaplain to our Holy Father the Pope, sends greeting."

"May you have hereafter the full enjoyment and the clear vision of the Sovereign Good, the object of all our desires!"

"We have understood, through the memorial our very clear sister has sent us, that you earnestly desire to see and possess in your monastery the Holy Face of our Savior, the guardianship of which is confided to us; that august Face which He bore upon earth when He lived amongst us, He, the most beautiful of the Children of men. You wish to enjoy this great privilege, in order that, by the contemplation of His divine features, your devotion may become livelier, and that the light of your souls may become more pure. Desiring with our whole heart to procure for you whatever is calculated to give you the grace of God in His world, and His eternal glory in the next, and wishing to

---

2. This recital is taken from a Notice published at Soissons in 1321, and which seems to be only an abridgment or a more considerable work published at Rheims in 1628, under the title or Rayons eclatants du Soleil de justice; with the approbation or MM. Porreau and Lallemand, doctors or the Faculty or that city.

accede, as far as in us lies, to the pious desire or our dear sister, we send you **a** copy of the Holy Face of which we have been speaking."

"Do not be astonished to find it discolored and blemished; those who live in a cool and mild climate have a white and delicate skin, while those who live in open fields have dark and bronzed complexions. It is the same with the Holy Face; the scorching sun of tribulations has discolored it, according to the expression of the Canticles, when our Savior was laboring in the field of the world for our Redemption. This is why we beg you to receive the holy Effigy with the veneration due to Him whose divine features it represents, treat it with devotion, delicacy and reverence, in order that the contemplation of it may be profitable to your souls. Remember us in your holy prayers and meditations, and firmly believe in the God whom you contemplate, whilst honoring and venerating his august Effigy."

"The personages from whom we have received it are Saints."

"Given in the year of grace **1249,** on the 3rd of July, the Monday after the feast of the holy Apostles Peter and Paul."

This precious picture, sent from Rome to the Nuns of Montreuil, still exists in the Cathedral of Laon.

It is portrayed in wax, upon a panel of pine wood, hollowed out like a basin and square in form.

Despite the ravages of lime, the Face of the Christ astonishes and impresses the beholder; the delicate features, of an oriental type, with full lips and serious expression, the deep set eyes, the uniform coloring of the divine Face, all give to the physiognomy a calm, grave, even severe expression. If it be contemplated, for but one moment only, it is difficult not to feel profound emotion.

We can easily imagine what was the joy experienced by the Abbess and the Nuns of Montreuil on receiving the divine Effigy. In obedience to the wishes expressed in the letter which accompanied it, they treated it with "devotion and reverence," redoubling their austerities and their love of penitence at the sight of so complete a model of charity and of expiation.

But such a treasure as this was not destined to remain hidden in the obscurity of a cloister. Providence was about to render it an object of respect to the whole country.

Dom Thierry de Brabant, the Cistercian Abbot of the monastery of the Dunes, in Flanders, having occasion to dedicate a new church, invited to the solemnity several of the neighboring bishops, and amongst others those of Therouanne and Tournay. In order to enhance the splendor of the ceremony, he begged the abbess of Montreuil to confide the Holy Face to him, in order that it might be solemnly exposed during the festival. Upon his promising that the separation from her beloved treasure should be of short duration, the Abbess gave her consent. Soon the news was spread far and wide, and from all the neighboring country the people flocked in crowds, not so much to assist at the ceremony of the dedication, as to see and honor the Holy Face, with the miraculous origin of which they were doubtless acquainted. Heaven recompensed the faith of the multitude. "During the night which preceded the solemnity, the Holy Face appeared surrounded by a miraculous light which cast its rays upon the whole of the adjacent country, and the next day, by looking at it for only a moment, the sick and infirm were instantly cured[3].

The tidings of these marvels, being swiftly promulgated, augmented the enthusiasm of the

---

3. **Dom Jean**-Baptiste **de** Laney: Historia Fusniacencis caenobii ordinis Cisterciensis, etc. Landuni, 1671.

faithful, and when the Abbot of the Dunes, after the dedication of his church, sent back the sacred Effigy according to his promise to Montreuil, the people eagerly hastened thither to contemplate it. There was, in fact, such a great concourse that, to satisfy the devotion of the pilgrims, the Nuns were obliged to expose the Holy Face in public on the high altar of their convent.

This pious movement increased with the lapse of years and gave birth to numerous associations. Thus, several confraternities were founded in honor of the Holy Face, amongst the principal of which were those of Mons, of Avesnes, of Quesnoy, of Landrecies and of Soignies. At Montreuil, the Nuns instituted a special feast for the Holy Face, which was fixed for the Sunday after the octave of the holy Apostles Peter and Paul, it being about that time that the venerable Effigy arrived from Rome. This feast was celebrated by a mass and a proper office. The confraternities of the towns of which we have just spoken went there in procession every year, which was the reason why, in order to satisfy the piety of all, two additional Sundays were added, which were subsequently styled the *"Sundays of the Processions."*

The people flocked to these annual reunions from Thierache, Flanders and Hainault, being attracted to Montreuil both from gratitude for favors which had been received and from the desire to obtain new graces.

During the epidemics which at a certain epoch were frequent and terrible in the country, the relics of the Saints were exposed, and carried in their reliquaries through the streets, and the Holy Face of Montreuil was also borne in procession through the cities invaded by the plague. Thus, on the 2nd of September 1495, it was taken to Saint-Quentin; from Saint-Quentin it was transported, on the 4th of the same month, to Moy, where it was placed in the chapel of the chatean, and many cures were obtained. On the 5th of September it made its appearance at La Fere, and on the 28th at Crepy-en-Laonnais. In 1496, Ribemont was attacked by a terrible pestilence, and the holy Picture was taken thither to give confidence and hope to the people in the midst of their trials.

These public calamities were followed by a space of about three centuries, during which period the country was almost unceasingly a prey to another scourge which was not less dreadful than the preceding ones. It was the war which France had to sustain successively against Burgundy, England and the Low Countries. More than ten times the Nuns of Montreuil were obliged to leave their convent and to abandon it to pillage or conflagration. This is the reason why there is a complete absence of information with regard to these religious down to the seventeenth century.

We know, however, that in 1628, the feast of the Holy Face was still celebrated at the convent with great pomp. The Confraternities affiliated to the original Confraternity had each of them their banner, with which they marched in good order, accompanying the miraculous Face, which was carried in procession under a canopy held by four priests. They halted at a pavilion in the cemetery, where a sermon was preached, and the concourse of people was so great, that the officers of the Duchy of Guise were obliged to be present in order to prevent disorder.

During the contests waged by France against the house of Austria, and in the midst of the invasions and bloody wars which carried rapine and conflagration into the countries of the North, the Religious of Montreuil retired at first lo Crepy-en-Laonnais, where they possessed a farm; then to the provostship of Chantrud, a dependency of the abbey of St. Martin of Tournay, and lastly to a hospital of a suburb of Laon, called Neuville. It was a consolation that they were able to preserve and carry away their dear Holy Face, without the precious

treasure having ever been taken from them in the midst of so many
other losses which they had to suffer. Their ancient abbey in Thierache
having been ruined and reduced to ashes, they called their new
residence by the name of "Montreuil-sous-Laon," the name which it
still bears, but which the people substitute often by that of the "Holy
Face."

Exposed to the piety of the faithful, the Effigy of the Savior
became anew the object of general veneration and the center of fresh
confraternities. Nevertheless, these confraternities did not come in
procession to Montreuil as those of former days had done, because of
the distance they had to traverse.

But the habit of making pilgrimages was still retained, and miracles
were granted as in former times. These miracles, if we may believe the
historians of the seventeenth and eighteenth centuries, were frequent
and numerous; minutes, pictures and other pieces of documentary
evidence preserved, either in the church or the abbey, furnished
authentic proof of the facts adduced. Unhappily we are deprived
of these documents, which were destroyed during the Revolution.
Notices dating from the years 1628 and 1722 state that there were
very few years in which some miraculous cures did not take place. At
the same time the worship of the Holy Face was encouraged by the
Sovereign Pontiffs. Thus Alexander VIII, in 1681; and Innocent XI,
in 1684, granted to it numerous indulgences.

As had been the case at Montreuil-Jes-Dames, the offices were
always celebrated with solemnity, and the faithful betook themselves
to them with the same confidence, above all, on the "procession
Sundays." The mass of the Holy Face and the complete office exist, as
printed at Laon in 1719. "The feast of the Holy Face," it is stated in
the preface to the book, "is celebrated on the Sunday which is nearest
to the octave of the holy Apostles Peter and Paul, and on the two

following Sundays when there is a plenary indulgence." This office, written for the Religious of Montreuil-sous-Laon, is approved by the Abbot of Citeaux; it is composed of passages taken from the Scriptures and the Fathers, and of an office of St. Veronica, which was celebrated at Saint-Eustache in Paris. The different editions of the office include the Litanies of the Holy Face, also taken from the Scriptures, and divided into three parts, probably for the use of the processions.

During the Revolution, in 1792, the Religious were driven away from their convent, and forced to abandon all which constituted its riches, the sacred ornaments, and above all, their ancient Holy Face. Transferred, at first, to the parish church of Neuville as a consequence of the demand made for it by the inhabitants, the precious Effigy was sacrilegiously taken away in 1793, and conveyed to the district of Laon. Serious dangers threatened it, but a faithful and courageous administrator of the district succeeded in withdrawing it from the notice of the agents of destruction by biding it under some papers at the bottom of a cupboard where it remained until 1795, when it was transported to Notre-Dame de Laon.

An episcopal ordinance published by the Bishop of Soissons, and dated the 8th of August 1807, recognizes its authenticity, and permits it to be solemnly exposed to the veneration of the faithful. It even appears that, in conformity with the said ordinance, the office of the Holy Face was celebrated during a certain period in the cathedral of Laon. Msgr. se Villele granted, in 1820, an indulgence of forty days to all those who should piously visit the venerable Effigy.

In 1838, the archpriest of Notre-Dame made praiseworthy efforts to withdraw it from its obscurity. It is still remembered that at Laon, in 1806, after a solemn triduum, preached with the greatest eloquence by the Rev. Father Lavigne, a question arose of reestablishing the pilgrimage and of honoring the precious Relic with special homage[4].

In 1880 and 1881, the procession, formerly made on the Sunday following the octave of the feast of St. Peter, took place in the cathedral of Laon, in the midst of a numerous assembly of the faithful. Everything then leads one to hope that the devotion to the Holy Face will resume the ancient splendor which, during so many centuries, it enjoyed in these localities.

---

4. The Rev. Father Lavigne was for a long-time acquainted with M. Dupont; there is no doubt that, at this period, the eloquent preacher was inspired with thoughts for which he was indebted to the holy Man of Tours.

THE HOLY FACE OF JAEN

Spain, a preeminently catholic nation, has at all times possessed in a superlative degree an appreciation of, and a delight in the great devotions of the Church. Spanish painters and sculptors have given expression, with striking and sometimes sublime force, to the torments of our Savior in His Passion. Pictured, or sculptured representations of the Holy Face, are very frequently to be found in churches and public museums, formed during the last thirty years from the spoils of different sacred edifices and monasteries. In addition to these works of art, Spain possesses several pictures of the Holy Face venerated with pious devotion as being reproductions of the veil of

Veronica. They are styled indifferently "Santa Faz, Cara de Dios," or "Santo Rostro."

The most celebrated of them all is, unquestionably, that of Jaen[1]. It has been venerated in the cathedral of the city from time immemorial. Placed in a splendid frame, enriched with emeralds, it may be easily seen, and a great number of engravings and of facsimiles of it are spread all over Spain and reverenced with great devotion by pious persons.

Spanish historians are not agreed as to the origin of this memorable picture. According to an ancient tradition, it dates from the times of the apostles, when St. Veronica herself was alive. It is believed to be one of the folds of her veil on which the Savior left His divine Effigy. Trustworthy authors are of opinion that the veil of Veronica was folded in three at the moment when the courageous Israelite presented it to the Man God, and that on each of the three folds was simultaneously impressed the ineffable lineaments of the sorrowful Face. These three several impressions, being afterwards separated from one another by Veronica, were each of them bestowed by her on different people. The first which she gave away is the Holy Face so piously preserved in Rome in the basilica of St. Peter at the Vatican. Veronica presented the second fold to the town of Zante, when, sailing from Judea to Italy, she disembarked at the island of Zante and became its apostle. It is not known what became of it, history has not been able

---

1. **This Notice has been compiled from private letters received from Spain, extracts from the Dictionary of Madoz and a pamphlet published al Jaen, under the title of Ajuntes historicos sobre el Movimento de la seda episcopal de Jaen y series correlativas de sus Orispos, by D. Ramon Rodriguez de Galvez: (Jaen, 1873.)**

to trace it. The third fold is that which is venerated at Jaen. It must have been given to St. Euphrasius, the apostle and first Bishop of the city, when he was sent from Rome by St. Peter, or his successors, and received the mission of evangelizing that part of Spain.

Pope Clement VII seems to confirm this tradition in a bull of the 20th of December 1529, by which he grants indulgences to the Church of Jaen. "It is therein stated that a pious and venerable Effigy of our Lord and Redeemer Jesus Christ, impressed upon a handkerchief, which Effigy our Savior Himself left to Veronica at the moment when He was ascending to Calvary, is preserved there and has been venerated from time immemorial." – "This Relic," it is added, "is held in great honor, and numerous pilgrims flock thither to visit it on the days when it is publicly exposed. "Jules II uses the same words in another bull which he granted to the same church in 1553. Acuna also repeats them and adds to them the litanies of the Holy Face, composed by Sancho d'Avila, "which are recited," he says, "at the time when the Holy Relic is exposed."

Brought from Rome to Spain by St. Ephrasius, the venerable Effigy remained at Jaen, where the Holy Bishop had fixed his seat, and where he suffered martyrdom at the hands of the infidels. After his death and later on, under the dominion of the Moors, it was carefully kept by the Christians, until the time when the city of Jaen was conquered and taken from the Mahomedans by the holy King Ferdinand.

It was in 1246, that this event occurred. The saintly Prince took possession of the sacred Effigy and carried it with him, as a standard in his military expeditions. One of the great historians of Spain, Marinaeus Siculus, when relating how the pious King, after he had conquered Jaen, also delivered Cordova and then Seville from the Mahomedan yoke, distinctly states that he bud with him the holy Effigy which was borne at the head of his armies. He was not able, before his death, to give back to Jaen the precious treasure which he had taken from the city, or else, if he left directions that it should be restored, his orders were not executed. The duty of making lawful restitution was reserved for Dom Nicolas de Biedna, who, being Archdeacon of Seville at the time, may have been informed of the intentions of King Ferdinand with respect to the Effigy. Having become Bishop of Jaco, he was afterwards named Vicar apostolic for the whole of Andalusia. This dignified post gave him, so the chroniclers of the period stale, sufficient authority to enable him to restore to his episcopal city the venerable relic of the Holy Face which had been its glory. It was in consequence brought back from the place where it had been detained, and placed in the cathedral of Jaen, which since that time has always kept possession of it.

We are, however, bound to state that more modern historians do not accept the tradition related above. They give to the fact which has been narrated quite another interpretation. According to them, Bishop Biedna, who filled the see or Jaen from **1368** to **1376,** demolished the mosque which had already been intended by the King to be converted into a cathedral. It was on that occasion that a translation of the Holy Face occurred, giving birth to the story of the restitution of the venerable Effigy. Moreover, according to them, King Ferdinand himself received it direct from Rome, at an epoch which is not known. The sovereign Pontiffs had, as may easily be understood, a direct interest in thus encouraging the pious Prince and the Christian armies, for which they procured in this manner the means of fighting the enemies of the faith under the eyes and before the Face of Christ. Pope Honorius **III,** or his predecessor, may have accordingly enriched Catholic Spain with the precious treasure at the request of its saintly King. For, in reality, say the same authors, the reliable and historical tradition does not go back further than the thirteenth century. The

Effigy, as it appears at present, is of the byzantine type, and must have been painted upon the original tissue while the primitive impression was still visible. Unhappily it has several times been retouched by different artists; it is therefore impossible to judge of what it originally was by means of its present aspect.

However, this may be, it is incontestable, according to the best Spanish authorities, that King Ferdinand held the Holy Face in profound veneration; and it appears no less unquestionable that the valiant monarch made use of it as his standard, and had it carried in battle at the bead of his armies, looking upon it as a guarantee of victory over the invaders _of his country and the enemies of the Christian name. It is also certain, and moreover admirably significative in regard to Catholic Spain, that the august Face of Christ presided over the last expulsion of the Moors from the country they had so long oppressed, and that it thus became the Labarum which drove the impious Mussulman beyond the extremities of the peninsula. Need we then be astonished if the Holy Face of Jaen has enjoyed so great celebrity throughout the whole of Europe, above all in the sixteenth century?

Its reputation has not diminished at the present day in the different provinces of Spain. The inhabitants of Jaen, in particular, profess the greatest veneration for their holy Effigy and esteem it a great honor to have it in their possession. It is placed in a shrine over the high altar of the principal chapel in the Cathedral. This shrine encloses another, made of beautifully wrought silver, which contains the holy Relic itself, set in a large golden frame, incrusted with precious stones of very considerable value, **the** whole being the gift of the Bishop of Jaen, Rodrigues Marin y Rubio.

The chapel in which the shrine is placed is locked with three keys which are kept by three Canons. There was formerly a confraternity attached to it, but it no longer exists.

The Holy Face is exposed to public veneration three times a year; on Good Friday, on the 15th of August, and on the Feast of the Assumption of the Blessed Virgin, to whom the Cathedral is dedicated; it is also exposed on the 1st of November, the festival of All Saints, in order to thank God for having preserved the city amidst the horrors of a terrible earthquake which occurred in 1755. On these occasions the Chapter chants certain passages which have relation to the Passion, and the Holy Face, with which the people are blessed in the interior of the Cathedral, is solemnly adored. This benediction is also given outside the church from four balconies, corresponding to the four cardinal points of the horizon. A great number of the faithful come to this ceremony and at the conclusion give their rosaries , medals and other objects of piety in order that they may touch the crystal which covers the sacred Effigy. When the 1st of November falls on a Saturday, which was the day of the week when the earthquake took place, the Holy Face remains exposed for the adoration of the faithful during the whole day until Compline. During the adoration, the Canons and clergy relieve each other every half hour.

In speaking of the Holy Face of Jaen, the glory of which is associated with the deliverance of Spain from the Mahomedan yoke, we may here mention an historical fact with which the annals of the Carmel of France furnish us and which is connected with the subject in question.

The Carmelites of the second convent, at Paris, possess a miraculous picture of the sorrowful Face of our Lord, which came from Spain under the following circumstances[2]. This holy Picture, of very ancient date and unknown origin, had fallen into the power of the Moors, who had taken it away from the Christians. Through hatred of our divine religion, the infidels attempted to pierce it and to slash it with a knife. On doing so, blood flowed forth from it in abundance and terrified them exceedingly. In their fear and fury, they threw the picture into the fire that it might be destroyed. The Holy Face, however, was proof against this fresh outrage and the flames respected it. Happily, it was rescued from the impious bands of the infidels, and during a long period the Church of Toledo preserved it as one of its most precious relics.

Now, on a certain occasion, Isabella of France, daughter of Henry IV and wife of Philip IV, King of Spain, being at Toledo, wished to see the treasure of the Cathedral, and the Cardinal Infante, who was the archbishop of the See, hastened to show her all its riches. The pious Queen was touched with only one of the pious objects shown to her. It was the impressive aspect of the ancient and miraculous picture of the Holy Face, which she immediately and urgently begged might he presented to her. The Cardinal consequently summoned the Chapter, and easily obtained its consent that the precious relic should be presented to the Queen. Isabella was delighted and never ceased to offer up before the Holy Face her homage of faith and piety. In her last moments she would not allow it to be taken down from her bedside, where she had placed it, and when she died, she left it to her daughter, Marie-Therese, entreating her to look upon the gift as an exceptional

---

2. **The details which follow are partly taken from the** Vie de Mme de Soyecourt, prieure du second Carmel de Paris, **rue de Vaugirard,** 86 (p. **LIX and** 104).

mark of her tenderness, seeing that she possessed nothing dearer to her in the whole world. Marie-Therese, having married Louis XIV, in 1660, came to France, and before her death (1683), left it as a legacy to the Convent of the Carmelites, which she had founded, and where the holy Picture has been safely kept down to the present day.

During the Revolution, in 1792, two commissaries of the district forced the Mother Prioress, to open to them the gates of the monastery, previous to expelling her and all the sisters. Invading the chapel, they began their work of destruction by breaking the reliquaries in order to seize anything precious which they might find and casting aside the holy Relics, to the great joy of the religious. Marie-Therese, their royal benefactress, had enriched the effigy of the Holy Face with a golden frame ornamented with diamonds. The commissaries seized these jewels, but they gave up the divine Effigy to the Superioress Mother Nathalie de Jesus, who placed it in a simpler frame and had its authenticity guaranteed by the Father Visitor, M. de Floirac, before he emigrated. After the reign of terror, the Prioress, having assembled the remaining portion of her daughters, established herself in another house where she died in 1798, leaving to the Religious, who succeeded her, this invaluable treasure thus providentially preserved in the midst of so many vicissitudes and storms. It will be easily understood that the holy Effigy is more than ever prized at the present day by the good Carmelites, who find their happiness in venerating it within their cloister, especially during Lent, and on the different festivals of the Passion celebrated at that holy season.

The following is a description of it with which we have been furnished. It is an oil painting on linen, oblong in form, being 30 centimeters long by 21 broad, preserved under glass in a wooden frame painted and gilt in the Moorish style. The complexion is pale and gray in hue; the countenance has a touching expression of suffering and of goodness, the whole face an aspect of gentleness and of calmness which is really divine. On the head is placed a great crown of interwoven thorns which entirely surround it. The lips are pallid; the hair and beard, of a warm chestnut color, merge gradually into the rest of the painting, which is almost completely in shade, the light being concentrated on the Face; the eyelids and the whites of the eyes are streaked with blood; the crown of thorns is of a greenish brown; the blood flows down and discolors the top of the forehead; some drops of blood stream down the face. The slashes made by the knives of the infidels, when they thrust them through it, may still be seen; the blood which miraculously flowed from it at the time seems to be coagulated, on each side, at the bottom of the picture, and mingled with little grains of sand. But nothing that be said of it can give any idea of the merit or this inestimable Effigy, which so vividly recalls the sufferings and the love of the Man God, the sovereign Restorer.

THE HOLY FACE OF OSA DE LA VEGA

Osa de la Vega is a small town in the diocese of Cuenga, in New Castile,
in the vicinity of the ancient and celebrated castle of Belmonte;
It has been the cradle of illustrious families and has always been
distinguished by the faith and probity of its inhabitants. But its great
privilege is that it preserves, in its parish church, as an object of pious

and popular worship, a miraculous effigy of the Holy Face, of which we propose to give a summary account[1].

In the beginning of the seventeenth century, there lived at Belmonte, a town in the neighborhood of Osa de la Vega, a holy priest named John Matilla who possessed a picture of the Holy Face, representing St. Veronica holding in her hands the veil on which was impressed the sorrowful lineaments of the Redeemer. How did he obtain this treasure? It is not known, but it is probable that he had received it from Rome. He attached very great value to it, and held it in such veneration that every evening, before betaking himself to sleep, he prostrated himself on his knees before it, and remained there an hour in adoration. He left it, at his death, to one of his relations, Isabelle del Corral y Matilla, wife of Jerome de la Torre, who lived at Osa de la Vega. Although she was a good Christian, the heiress of this precious treasure did not seem at first to attach any great value to it. However, she took it away with her to Belmonte and placed it in one of the rooms of her house, without being attracted to the Holy Face by any special devotion, as she herself declared later on. No one then suspected the designs of Providence in regard to it.

It was on Holy Thursday the 24th of March 1644. Towards six o'clock in the evening, at the moment when the inhabitants of Osa de la Vega had congregated together in the church in order to have the sorrowful Passion and death of the Savior explained to them, a touching and inexplicable prodigy took place in the house of Jerome

---

1. This recital is extracted and translated from the Historia del santissimo Rostro de Jesus que se venera en la ville de Osa de la Vega, by D. Pedro de la Torre, presbitero .. Madrid, 1874. (Pamphlet of **117** pages.)

de la Torre. Isabelle del Corral, his wife, had gone into the room where
the holy Effigy was, of which we have spoken, in order to get a tunic
for a brother of the "congregation of the Blood of Jesus Christ."

On entering the room, she was dazzled by an extraordinary light.
Filled with astonishment, she proceeded to examine more closely what
it was that had struck her. Oh prodigy! she perceived that the vivid
rays of light she had beheld were streaming from the holy Effigy
placed in the room; she moreover saw drops of sweat running down
it in abundance, as she affirmed un oath, in the inquiry which was
afterwards instituted respecting the wonderful event. In her presence
the adorable Face of Jesus sweated blood and water, as it had done in
the garden of Olives; she distinctly beheld tears flowing from the eyes
of the divine Effigy, and drops of blood running down from the head
where it had been wounded by the crown of thorns.

Without, strange to say, feeling troubled at the sight, she left the
room to give to a little girl the tunic she had come for. On returning,
she again beheld, for the second lime, the same prodigy; only the
sweat was still more abundant, whilst from the forehead and along
the cheeks of the Holy Face drops of blood and water ran down
upon the beard. Then, touched and overwhelmed with admiration in
presence of so extraordinary an occurrence, the pious woman could
no longer restrain herself; she hastened away from the room to tell
others what she had seen. The tidings spread on all sides, like an electric
spark, amongst the inhabitants of the country. They hastened to the
spot, and the whole multitude, filled with emotion and enthusiasm, .
proclaimed aloud the miracle.

Together with cries of enthusiasm were mingled tears and sighs
and all the signs of deep compunction. Information was given of the
event to the Rev. Father Michel Conde, a Religious of the monastery
of Santa Cruz of Villaescusa de Haro. It was eight o'clock in the

evening when he reached the house. Approaching the holy Picture, he examined the sweat which covered the divine Face. In order to assure himself that it was a fact, and to remove all possibility of illusion, he took a lighted taper and examined the sweat and blood attentively and leisurely. He then saw that they were drops of about the size of the seed of a pomegranate. Having taken some of these drops into his consecrated hands, he was able to convince himself that from the Holy Face was indeed flowing a real sweat of blood and water. The prudent, grave Religious also observed that from the eyes of the holy Picture two drops of blood had issued, which in the space of one hour and a quarter, flowed clown the sacred cheeks. He, moreover, observed that the head and the locks of hair were covered with a kind of dew of sweat, that the Face was at one moment suffused with color like that of a person in suffering, and that the next moment it became pale as though it were under the influence of some internal agony; that the eyes were sad and the lips swollen, and that from them flowed down drops of sweat. After having given an account of the miracle to the parish priest, Alonso Serrano y Guijarro, who had not been able to come to the house until after the divine office, he decided, to calm the extreme agitation of the faithful, that the holy Effigy should be taken to the parish church. He then had it placed in the Baptistery, and, for greater security, he himself kept the key of the chapel.

On Holy Saturday, the faithful being assembled in the church at the hour when the divine office is celebrated, the parish priest, clothed in his sacerdotal vestments and accompanied by the clergy, went to the chapel of the baptismal fonts, where the precious Effigy had been placed, that he might bless the fonts as usual. At the moment when he was repeating the first prayer, Alonso Serrano perceived that the holy Effigy was covered with a sweat which was very apparent. But he behaved as though he had not observed it, to moderate the enthusiasm of the assistants, who had seen the miracle, and proceeded with the blessing of the fonts. When the office was terminated, he asked for some corporals, with the object of making himself still more certain of the miracle and of giving undoubted evidence of it to the astonished crowd. Placing himself on bis knees before the altar, on which was the miraculous Effigy, he called two alcades to come forward and begged them to stand upon a bench, in order that they might be able to observe more closely the miracle which had taken place. In presence of the civil authorities, the priest Alfonso wiped away numerous drops of sweat, and two of blood with which the corporals were stained and marked. He then proceeded to wipe away the other drops. The priests who were present and the faithful got up successively upon the bench, and thus they were all of them able to give testimony to the miraculous sweat, on seeing the corporals damp and stained with the blood and the water which the parish priest had wiped away unlit the Holy Face remained completely dry. The people then retired and the priest Alfonso closed the chapel, using the same precautions as he had done on Holy Thursday.

In order to perpetuate the remembrance of this miracle, it was resolved that the corporals should be preserved with reverence and veneration in the tabernacle of the altar of the Rosary. Since then, they have been placed in that of Our Lady of the Nativity. In 1862, by order of Msgr. the Bishop, Dom Miguel Faya y Rico, they were removed to the tabernacle of the altar of the Holy Face, where they are piously preserved in a small case.

On the afternoon of the same Holy Saturday, about two o'clock, certain persons who were grievously disappointed that they had not been able to witness the miracle which had taken place in the morning, came to the church to worship the holy Effigy. Then, for the third lime, the Face of Jesus, appeared to become wet and to sweat in almost the same manner as on the previous occasions. The priest Alfonso, coming to the chapel just at this juncture, opened the door, went in, and, as before, wiped away the drops of sweat with some corporals.

A commission was then named by the Bishop of Cuenca, Msgr. Henriquez Pimentel, and commanded. to draw up a verbal process of the fact which had occurred. Judges were appointed, and a synod was held on the 23rd of March 1645, in the palace and under the superintendence of Msgr. Pimentel. Enquiry having been made, it was unanimously declared, and stated in accordance with the due canonical regulations, that the sweat of blood and water of the holy Effigy was "a miracle worked by the Almighty, and that, consequently, the venerable Face of Christ our Lord was a treasure of inestimable value of which the province of Cuenca had grounds to congratulate itself, and that it ought to endeavor to put it to profit in order to the greater glory of the divine Majesty and the exaltation of the Catholic faith."

Sharing these convictions· and desirous of favoring the devotion towards this holy Picture, the Sovereign Pontiff Clement X, by a bull dated the 14th of December 1674, granted great spiritual favors to the chapel of the Holy Face, and amongst others the privilege of a perpetual jubilee. A confraternity in honor of the most Holy Face of Jesus was founded on the 25th of March 1676, and another bull of the same Pope granted to it numerous indulgences. A feast of the Holy Face was celebrated on the Sunday during the octave of the Nativity of the Blessed Virgin. The feast of the Immaculate Conception, the feast of the holy Name of Jesus on, the second Sunday of the Epiphany, Holy Thursday, and the feast of the Precious Blood were also considered to be feasts proper to the confraternity. At the hour of death, such members of the confraternity as had been constant in wearing a scapular of the Holy Face, might gain a special plenary indulgence; numberless graces are related, wherewith God recompensed the devotion of the inhabitants of Osa de la Vega for their dear and venerable Effigy.

Nevertheless, at the present day, it appears that the pilgrimage of which it was the object is little more than a memory. But the confraternity, which had also become a thing of the past, has lately been revived, and it is said that it makes great progress in the Philippine islands. An interesting pamphlet was published at Madrid in 1874, entitled the History of the Holy Face of Osa de la Vega; it is from it that we have compiled the preceding abstract. One of the French Dominican Fathers, who have taken refuge at Belmonte, permits us to add the following details- "The miraculous Effigy is inexpressibly beautiful; it is a work of art of great value. The Face of the Christ, its eyes bathed in tears and blood, is so touching in its expression, that it is impossible to look at it without emotion. I have had the indescribable happiness of touching with my hands the sacred linen which was used to wipe away the sweat of blood. The corporals are as fresh as though they had been used but yesterday; so perfect a preservation seems to be little less than miraculous. They are kept in the tabernacle of the altar of the Holy Face, and the same homage as that paid to the most Blessed Sacrament itself is rendered to them[2]."

---

2. Letter from the Rev. Father Brochard. Belmonte , 9th of October 1883.

THE HOLY FACE OF ALICANTE

Alicante is a Spanish town in the southern part of the province of Valentia, and is situated upon the Mediterranean coast, where it possesses a commercial and much-frequented port. Very near to the town, in a monastery of Poor Clares, known by the name of the convent of St. Veronica, there is a beautiful and celebrated effigy of the Holy Face, which is the object of a great popular devotion. The veneration paid to this ancient Effigy is attached to the fact we are about to relate.

In the year 1489, an excessive drought was so prevalent in Alicante and the neighborhood, that all the fruits of the earth were menaced with complete destruction, and it was then that the priest of a rural parish was seized with the idea of making a solemn procession from his church to the convent of the Observantine Minims. In this procession, inspired as it was by a spirit of penitence, a Holy Face, copied from the one at Rome known as the veil of Veronica, was carried amidst public prayers in which a great concourse of people joined. A Religious of the Minimes, Father Villa Franca by name, was charged with the pious and honorable task of bearing it in his arms. "All at once[1] the holy Effigy became so heavy, that the Friar's arms were obliged to be supported. Moreover, when he had ascended an elevated spot in order that the whole assemblage might plainly see the Effigy, it was remarked, the day being perfectly serene, that a tear, more limpid than crystal, was falling from the right eye. At the sight of this miracle, the whole multitude with one voice implored the divine mercy." Just at that moment, Father Benedict de Valence; a Franciscan Monk whose sanctity was held in great repute, and who was titular preacher to the King of Spain, as well as provincial of Aragon, made his appearance. "The church being too small to contain so great a multitude, the Father began to preach in the open air a most touching sermon, and at the conclusion of it asked his hearers to meet him again on the following day and in the same place. It happened that the next day was a Friday, and during the sermon, the sky, which the day before had been perfectly serene, was

---

1. **Partly** extracted **from** the Palmier seraphique, vol. **IV, 15th** of **April. A** "Romancero" of the **Holy** Face **has been recently published;** it is a **long epic poem in verse** upon "The miraculous **Effigy** venerated **in** the **monastery of** St. Veronica, **in** the neighborhood of **Alicante."** The notes and explanations placed at the end of the poem have **furn**ished **us with some valuable historical** details.

suddenly veiled with thick clouds. Father Benedict, who was holding in his hands the holy Effigy and elevating it in the air, was suddenly plunged into an ecstasy. At the same moment two other Holy Faces, exactly similar, appeared in the midst of the clouds. When the preacher came to himself, his ecstasy having ceased, he gave the blessing to the people with the Holy Face he was holding in his hands. Then the two other representations which had mysteriously shown themselves in the sky disappeared, and the cloud, dividing itself into four portions disposed like a cross, shed forth an abundant rain which restored to the earth its freshness and gave new life to its productions."

Another time, when the man of God was showing this same Effigy to his hearers who were imploring aloud the divine mercy and forgiveness of their sins, a great cross of various colors, similar to a rainbow, was observed lo be suspended above the Father's cross.

These miracles inspired the inhabitants of Alicante with great devotion to the Holy Face of our Lord, and the blessed Benedict prevailed on the city to found a monastery of Poor Clares, in the place where it had been seen to weep. Subsequently, a splendid church was built, and it is there that the precious Effigy is still preserved and that it is publicly venerated. It would take too long to enumerate the miracles of all kinds which have rendered this worship more and more popular. Suffice it to say that in maladies, droughts, inundations and other scourges which have visited the country, the citizens of Alicante have never had recourse to their Holy Face without experiencing its powerful protection.

The faithful were accustomed to visit it in its sanctuary on the Fridays in Lent. Every year about the 17th of March, a triduum of feasts was celebrated with indescribable solemnity. So great, in the eighteenth century, was the renown of the Sacred Face of Alicante, that there was not a ship in the port, coming from the East, or on the point of sailing thither, which did not salute the Picture with a salvo of artillery. This example was more than once imitated by protestant English and Dutch sailors. At the present day the captains of merchant vessels raise their flag when they come in sight of the monastery. The people of the country continue to visit the church and often go there barefooted; they also have masses said in honor of the Holy Face and in gratitude for the benefits obtained by its means.

The annual procession always takes place with the magnificence and pomp which Spain knows so well how to bestow upon religious ceremonies when the civil authorities join in them together with the clergy. The Holy Face is then uncovered, hymns are sung in its honor, and it is solemnly shown to the people. It is afterwards carried triumphantly along the streets of the city under a splendid dais held by eight priests, and it is the highest dignitary amongst the clergy who hears it in his hands. In **1859,** the Bishop performed the function, walking on fool in the midst of an edified and ravished crowd.

Enclosed in a very rich reliquary in the form of a monstrance, it is placed between two plates of crystal united together by an admirably wrought band of silver and surrounded by a graceful wreath composed of eight heads of angels. The lance, the sponge and the other instruments of the Passion surmount the whole, and seem to indicate that the Holy Face itself, spite of the glory and beauty which shine from it, bears the signet of suffering.

THE HOLY FACE OF LUCCA

At Lucca, in Tuscany, the name of "Volto Santo," Holy Face, is given to a wooden crucifix of which the face, wonderful in its beauty, is the object of public veneration. During eleven hundred years the worship of the "Volto Santo" has subsisted at Lucca: six years ago (1882), the eleventh century of its translation was solemnized with both religious and civil pomp. The following is, in a few words, an account of the origin and the history of this memorable effigy[1].

It is attributed to the pious Israelitish Senator of whom the Gospel makes mention under the name of Nicodemus, and who was at first a secret disciple of Jesus, until, instructed and enlightened by the Divine Master, he openly followed in His footsteps, and, together with Joseph of Arimathea, took Him down from the Cross after His death and gave Him the honors of burial. Driven from Jerusalem by the enemies of the Savior, deprived of his title, and despoiled of his goods, he was reduced to extreme poverty and took refuge at Ramla, a little town situated between Jerusalem and Joppa. It was there that he died. This is the tradition which has been constantly preserved in Palestine from time immemorial. It is a fact that the Franciscans possess at Ramla, a town of **3,500** inhabitants, a very ancient convent where they exercise hospitality towards pilgrims, and in which an oratory is shown bearing the name of St. Nicodemus.

Tradition also relates, and all ancient and modern historians who have written upon the Holy Land equally attest, that the celebrated representation of Christ crucified, known under the name of "the Holy Face" was sculptured there. It is venerated in the principal

---

1. This Notice is a faithful, although very incomplete, summary of an extremely interesting pamphlet, which is itself only the abridgment or a learned ancient work. It was published on the occasion of the feasts of the centenary, under the title or Nolizie storiche del Santo Vollo di Lucca, per il sacerdote Almerico Guerra, canonico onorario della Metropolitana Luchese (1881).

church at Lucca, and according to the expression of Pope Innocent VIII, renowned throughout the whole world.

In his solitude and exile, the pious disciple, in order to reproduce the form of the Christ, had only to recall to mind his most recent remembrances. He had but lately rendered the last offices to the adorable body of the Redeemer, he had touched Him with his hands, taken Him down from the Cross, and laid Him in His sepulcher. The features of the Divine Crucified Savior, bruised and disfigured by suffering and death, had remained profoundly impressed upon his memory. Recalling to recollection the words which he had listened to from the month of the Savior in his memorable interview with Him- As Moses lifted up the serpent in the desert, so must the Son of Man be lifted up ... , he endeavored to reproduce, by means of sculpture, the mystery of the Man God suspended from the Cross, and to represent Him as he had seen Him with his own eyes. He then set himself to work. In accordance with an old custom, prevalent amongst the Jews, who were obliged, no matter to what rank they belonged, to practice a manual trade, he had, spite of his senatorial dignity and distinguished birth, employed himself in sculpture all his life, and he was therefore proficient in the art.

He employed a piece of oak to make the cross, and a cedar of Lebanon wherewith to reproduce the body of Jesus. Tradition relates that having terminated the Crucifix, with the exception of the head, the able artist found himself arrested by the difficulty of carving that portion of the divine Body, though he had doubtless present to his mind and in his heart the ineffaceable features of his well-beloved Master. The pious sculptor, following the example of the Saints, who, in like case, had recourse to fervent prayer, prostrated himself on his knees and, whilst prolonging his secret intercourse with God, he suddenly fell into a peaceful sleep. Hardly had he awakened from it, than he rose and hastened to contemplate his **work.** With what astonishment and emotion was he not overpowered, when **he** found that **the face** had been finished **by** the **hand** of **an** angel who had adapted it to the remaining portion of the body. **It** was admira**bly carved, vividly representing** as it did the **Majesty, the** sorrow and the mercy of the Man God upon the Cross. Filled with joy and at the same time greatly moved and affected, Nicodemus prostrated himself on his knees before the beloved crucifix which so perfectly reproduced to him what he remembered of the ineffable face of his adorable Master. He placed **it** in a post of honor in his dwelling, and summoned all the faithful, who, **having** been dispersed by the persecution, had taken refuge in the town and the neighborhood, to come and venerate it.

Such is, in substance, the tradition relative to the origin of the "Volto Santo." Now it will be well to bear in mind that there are in the East traditions supremely worthy of respect. "If there be anything," says Chateaubriand, "proved upon earth, it is the authenticity of the Christian traditions of Jerusalem." This remark specially applies to the tradition which looks upon Nicodemus as the sculptor of the crucifix, the so called "Holy Face" of Lucca. It has the authority of a grave and trustworthy tradition, and consequently has an historical value which it would be presumptuous to reject or to contest. Consequently a crowd of writers, deeply versed in sacred history and in the laws of criticism, do not hesitate to admit it; amongst them may he named Pope Innocent XI, Cardinal Baronius, Dom Calmet, Bellarmine, Paleoti, Gretzer, Henschenius, Mansi, Muratori, etc. These weighty authors will doubtless suffice to enable our readers to give full credence to what has been stated above on the subject.

We will now proceed to describe the Holy Effigy. The cross, of the usual form, is 4 meters 34 centimeters high, and 2 meters 75 centimeters broad. The thickness of the wood is 7 centimeters and the breadth 27 centimeters. The wood is of oak, dyed black. The Christ, sculptured in cedar wood, is fastened to the cross by four nails. The heads of the nails which pierce the hands are small, whilst those which fasten the feet cannot be perceived on the upper side, it is only the place where they have been driven in which can be seen. The body is larger than the natural size, measuring 2 meters 25 centimeters from the head to the sole of the foot. The venerable head of the Savior is a little inclined to the right and bent forward as though to receive the prayers of all who have recourse to Him and to look upon them in mercy. On first beholding it, reverence is the chief emotion with which His face inspires the spectator; it even seems to be terrible in its aspect, but if it be contemplated more attentively, it will soon be perceived that it wears an expression of majesty and suffering united with sweetness and gentleness which inspires an emotion of love. That the face of the Redeemer should have been at once sweet and majestic, majestic and terrible to the wicked, sweet and amiable to the good, seems to be most natural. St. Catherine, writing to a lady at Lucca, says to her when speaking of the Holy Face— "Go to the most sweet Cross! Its Face looks lovingly and gently on the good." Now, on a certain occasion, it was at the commencement of the present century, - the Holy Face had been uncovered that it might be shown to a great personage. As soon as he had looked at it, he cried out, being seized with terror, - "Hide it, hide it." It was the same Face, only there was a great difference between St. Catherine of Sienna and the worldly personage in question.

The hair of the "Volto Santo" is black, divided down the middle after the manner of the Nazarenes, and falling abundantly upon the shoulders. The beard, of the same color, is neither short nor long, as becomes a man still young; it leaves the chin uncovered and descends in two separate tufts. One thing worthy of remark is that the Effigy represents Jesus, not dead, but living and suffering; the eyes are open and the lips, which have fallen a little apart, seem to move and to give to the Effigy a marvelous expression of life. There is no crown of thorns, which is in conformity with ancient custom; Jesus was not indeed crucified without the crown, only the primitive Christians preferred to recall to mind, not the ignominy, but the glory of Him who had ascended the Cross to save the world and to draw all hearts to Him. The face is Oriental in type, the Savior in this respect resembling his brethren, who were of the children of Israel. Another peculiarity distinguishes the "Crucifix" of Lucca; and that is that, with the exception of the face, the whole of the figure is clothed. Nicodemus, through respect, would not represent the body of his divine Master in a naked state; be therefore sculptured a garment which entirely covers the figure. Moreover, it was customary in the early ages of the Church thus to represent Christ on the Cross.

During a long period of time, the sacred treasure left by Nicodemus at his death was carefully kept in the most private part of his habitation, that it might not be discovered by the Israelites who bore the Effigies of Christ and of the Saints in mortal hatred. Under the Pontificate of Adrian I, and the reign of Charlemagne, pilgrimages to the Holy Land began to be set on foot. Amongst the pilgrims of a certain epoch was a Piedmontese Bishop, Gualfredo, by name, who sojourned for a long time in Palestine and who had a revelation of the mysterious effigy of the Redeemer. He consequently formed the design to take it from the infidels and to transport it to Italy. He was aided in this projects by succor sent from on high. For he found, as though by accident, on the borders of the sea, a skiff in which he placed the crucifix which, impelled over the waves, arrived on the shores of Tuscany, in front of the port of Lucca. Vessels, seeing that it was without a pilot and destitute of a rudder, attempted to seize the boat, but the mysterious skiff escaped from their pursuit with supernatural swiftness. The Archbishop or Lucca, being informed of what had happened, betook himself there at the head of his clergy, when the skiff immediately delivered itself up into his hands, and the precious treasure became, through the Divine will, the possession of the city of Lucca, formerly evangelized by St. Paulin, a disciple of St. Peter. The cathedral was for a long time dedicated to St. Martin, the illustrious Bishop of Tours.

The Bishop of Lucca constructed, in a place adjacent to his cathedral, a chapel in which the "Volto Santo" was placed. From that moment the devotion of the people towards it increased daily, and miracles were so greatly multiplied, that it was found necessary to transport the holy Relic to the Cathedral itself, where it still remains. Soon its celebrity became universal; it attracted to it thousands of pilgrims of all ranks of life, not only belonging to Italy, but to all the countries in the world.

The affluence of people produced marvels of another kind, those namely of catholic charity. According to the chronicles of the time, Lucca and its suburbs numbered not less than twenty hospitals, destined to receive gratuitously the pilgrims of the "Volto Santo." In the middle of the thirteenth century the hospitals of the diocese, having their own revenues and patrimony, rose to fifty. The pilgrim, as soon as he arrived in the territory of Lucca, was certain of immediately finding a house of refuge where he could rest if he were tired, obtain food if he were hungry, and be nursed if he were sick. He had no need to be afraid that he would have to remain at night alone in a desert place, for on his path he would be sure to meet with a friendly hand to lead him to a hospitable house. A chaplain was stationed all day long under "the porch" of the church, that he might be always ready to bestow upon the pilgrims the offices of sacerdotal charity.

When descending the mountains, on coming from Florence, torrents and impassible bogs had often to be traversed. There was, consequently, formed a society of Religious called "Brothers," or "Knights of St. James of the Heights," because they met at first in a little church dedicated to St. James, the patron of pilgrims. They were the first who bad the honor of constituting an order of chivalry, which has served as a model to all subsequent societies of the same kind. These Knights of the Heights constructed bridges, or made boats for traversing the torrents, rivers and marshes. They carried the traveler on their shoulders, often waiting for him in dangerous places leading him to the hospital, and administering restoratives to him. Towards evening the convent bell began to ring and continued to do so until it had become quite dark, to give notice of the proximity of the hospital; it was this bell which was known by the name of "the bell of the wanderer."

The city of Lucca was, for a long time, the capital of one of those small Italian republics which were formerly so flourishing and so celebrated. It had consequently its own form of government, and as this government was eminently Christian, the people of Lucca gave a religious character to their political and civil life. They were the first to stamp their coin with sacred effigies, on one side bearing the Holy Face and on the obverse that of St. Martin and sometimes of St. Peter. It was only at our own epoch, the 26th of April **1858,** that these effigies were suppressed by a decree of the government of Tuscany, to which Lucca then belonged. The day when this law passed was looked upon as a fatal day, and in fact, just a year afterwards, on the very same day, the Grand Duke was dethroned, and quit Florence and Tuscany never to return there.

The seals of the state of Lucca also bore the effigy of the Holy Face on one side, and on the obverse St. Martin on horseback with his lance at rest. Acts and contracts were drawn up in honor of the Holy Face. The law condemned blasphemers of it to the most severe penalties. Finally, although a republic, the Luccese had elected the Volto Santo to be their king, in right of which there was placed upon its forehead a rich and splendid royal crown. The feast of the Holy Face was the national feast; it was celebrated, clown to the end of the twelfth century, on Easter Tuesday, and after that epoch on the 14th of September. This did not however prevent St. Martin from having a feast of the rite of the first class, as patron of the diocese. On Good Friday and the 14th of September, prisoners were set free in the name and in honor of the Holy Face. These facts sufficiently prove how greatly the inhabitants of Lucca loved and honored their holy Effigy and how Jesus Christ had really become their King.

A confraternity of the Volto Santo was established at a very early period. It had its rules and a vast organization, which rendered it at once a religious and civil institution whose object was to favor, by all possible means, the devotion to the Holy Face. Its meetings were held in the Cathedral on the third Sunday of every month. They were announced in advance, by special messengers who went from house to house in the different parishes, and they were terminated by a solemn procession in the neighborhood of the church. In the sixteenth century the Confraternity was merged in that of the Holy Sacrament which was very ancient, and which then assumed the title of the "Confraternity of the Holy Sacrament and of the Holy Face." It had a double object, the first of which was to provide everything that was necessary for celebrating, with due pomp, the offices of Holy Thursday and of Good Friday, and the second the procession on the feast of Corpus Christi. In 1837, the Archbishop of Lucca reestablished the Confraternity of the Holy Face; some years afterwards it already numbered ten thousand associates.

From Lucca the devotion of the "Volto Santo" spread not only throughout the principal towns of Italy, but also throughout the whole of Europe, it may be even said throughout the whole world, and everywhere it flourished in an extraordinary manner. To speak only of France, in Paris above all, the Holy Face was designated by the name of the "St. Voult" of Lucca, or "St. Vandele." The mother of SL. Louis, Blanche of Castile, had **a** great devotion for the Holy Face of Lucca; it was at her command **that t**he celebrated history of Leboino upon the "Volto Santo" was translated, and this translation was placed in the National Library, where **it is** probably still to be found. In a very ancient Processional of Paris there is a special commemoration of the "Volto Santo;" it was made on Holy Thursday and it had relation to the outrages inflicted by the Jews and the Roman soldiers on the adorable Face of the Savior.

At the epoch of the cholera, in 1835, the Luccese who had escaped the scourge attributed their preservation to the "Volto Santo" and offered to it as an ex-voto a golden lamp, of the weight of 24 lbs. Nor have they forgotten the visit of Pius IX, in 1857, **a** circumstance which they took care to recall to the recollection of the holy Pontiff when they presented to him, in 1871, a superb fac-simile of their celebrated Effigy. Finally, in the month of May 1883, when the eleventh centenary of the arrival of the crucifix of Nicodemus occurred, the whole of Lucca gave itself up during three days to the celebration of a religious and civil festival, the magnificence of which recalled the most splendid epochs of its bygone history.

A chapel in the middle of the Cathedral is destined to the Cri1cifix. It is a small edifice in white marble, round in form, and admirably sculptured by an ancient artist, belonging to the country. There is an altar in it where mass is said, and the altar piece of which contains the reliquary. In order to see and venerate the Relic on days other than those of the public exhibition of it, it is necessary to have the permission of the Archbishop and the Chapter. This permission was granted to us in October 1886. This private exhibition was, however, accompanied by a certain degree of solemnity. It was necessary to wait until the close of day and until the doors of the basilica were closed. Then a canon habited in a surplice and accompanied by two clerks carrying lighted tapers, uncovered the holy Crucifix, and after several liturgical prayers permitted us to contemplate and to venerate it at our leisure. Its aspect appeared to us to be in accordance with the description already given of it. Seen in front, it has an expression full of sweetness and gentleness, but looked at in profile it is severe and menacing. This act of piety is not accomplished without the soul being filled with profound emotion of which the remembrance is ineffaceable.

The remains of Nicodemus and those of Gamaliel are preserved and venerated at Pisa, where an altar is dedicated to them in the Duomo. We celebrated mass there when returning from our journey to Sotero (in the diocese of Alexandria), to which place we had been sent by the metropolitan Chapter of Tours in order to receive relics of St. Perpet, one of our most illustrious Bishops, and to whom we owe the first basilica of the great miracle worker of the Gauls, St. Marlin.

THE HOLY FACE OF
TOURS

The holy Effigy honored at Tours with a special worship in the chapel known by the name of the "Oratory of the Holy Face," deserves to be mentioned as being one of the most celebrated copies or the veil of Veronica.

It dates its origin from the season of Lent, in the year 1851. Some years previously the Prioress of the Carmelites at Tours had confidentially imparted to M. Dupont the sacred communications made by our Lord to Sister Marie de Saint-Pierre respecting the mysteries of the Holy Face. On becoming acquainted with them, he was seized with an ardent love for the Divine Face, making it his favorite subject of devotion, and delighting to render it the topic of conversation with his friends, whether priests or pious laymen. The Prioress of Carmelites had. received from the Benedictines of Arras three fac-similes of the celebrated picture so jealously preserved at Rome in the basilica of St. Peter of the Vatican. To these representations were attached certificates of authentication. They had been engraved at the period when during the exile of Pius IX, at Gaeta, the features of the august Effigy impressed upon the veil of Veronica had, through a most astonishing miracle, suddenly appeared to become animated with life. The Mother Prioress of Carmel felt that it would give the servant of the Holy Face no small pleasure if she were to offer him two of the copies which had come from the Eternal city, and she accordingly did so.

M. Dupont, on receiving them, gave one of these copies to the Lazarist fathers of Tours, to be placed in the chapel set apart for the nocturnal adoration; the other be kept for himself and hung it up in his drawing-room. The day that he put it there was Wednesday in Holy Week. In placing it in so conspicuous a position, in the most frequented portion of his house, it being the room where he was accustomed to receiving his visitors and friends, he wished, by so striking a mark of religious homage, to render it still more impressive. He, moreover, lighted a lamp before it, similar to those placed before the Blessed Sacrament in churches, destined to burn without interruption night and day.

This act of piety of the servant of God quickly attracted observation. He himself delighted to draw the attention of anyone who chanced to visit him to the holy picture, proposing to his ordinary visitors that they should kneel down before it and pray, and to the sick that they should anoint themselves with the oil of the lamp: Graces were at once obtained, and miracles worked. It was the beginning of a domestic and private worship, which M. Dupont's ecclesiastical superiors authorized by their silence, and which many priests and faithful ardently embraced.

During the twenty-five years which elapsed, before the death of M. Dupont, his drawing-room, enriched and sanctified by the holy Picture, was the center of constant pilgrimage in honor of the sorrowful Face of the Man God. Little by little, numbers of persons, not only belonging to Tours and the neighboring dioceses, but also to all parts of France and even to foreign countries, flocked thither. Physical miracles and conversions were almost daily obtained and took place in sight of the public. In the midst of this supernatural movement, he who was called the Holy Man of Tours, humbly sought to efface himself; he rejoiced in and willingly gave praise to the divine power' manifested in the miracles; he even preserved with jealous care the medical certificates and other documents attesting the graces which had been obtained. But he did so only because he saw in them a confirmation of the heavenly communications made to Sister Saint-Pierre, and a striking proof that our Lord willed that this glorification of His Holy Face should be a providential means of reparation for the blasphemies and profanations of modern society.

On all sides, in imitation of the servant of God, the desire was manifested to have in a church, a chapel, or private oratory, copies of the veil of Veronica sent from Rome and similar to that of M. Dupont. At the same time, in the midst of the confidence and the veneration felt towards them, it was always understood that it was right to make a distinction and establish a difference between them and the picture preserved in the Oratory at Tours. That was in the eyes of all the supreme "Miraculous Picture;" it was willingly styled "the Holy Face of M. Dupont;" it was to it that prayers and recommendations were especially addressed; and it was from the lamp burning before it that the oil was supplied for the anointings used for the sick. It would be difficult to enumerate the multitude of miracles of which it has been the source. The process commenced for the cause of the Holy Man reveals every day something new.

On the death of M. Dupont, in 1876, his drawing-room, having been canonically transformed into a public chapel, the august Effigy remained in the same place where the servant of God had put it, namely on the right-hand side of the altar which has been constructed there. A rich frame, the gift of the Christian mothers of Tours, and in addition to the old lamp, four new lamps similar to those of the tomb of St. Peter at Rome, were placed before it, enhancing the simplicity of its primitive surroundings. It continues to be the object of a worship no longer private in its nature, but public and solemn, and diffused throughout nearly the whole world. For it identifies itself with the homage of faith and of reparation approved by the Archbishops of Tours and the Sovereign Pontiff Leo XIII, with regard to the divine Face of our Lord. The privilege of a great catholic archconfraternity and the concession of numerous indulgences have recently given to it the highest possible sanction. A supernatural attraction also adds to the respect inspired by the sacred Picture; it is the secret and irresistible emotion which the sight of it produces on all who contemplate it with some degree of attention -- priests, religious, men of God and simple laymen, wise men and ignorant, worldly persons and sinners, have been seen to enter the Oratory, as though by chance or from mere curiosity, and, on perceiving the sorrowful expression of the Face of Christ, have felt themselves to be attracted towards it, to be touched and affected sometimes to tears. A fervent prayer and a good confession have frequently been the unexpected result in the case of several amongst them.

Such, then, is the worship rendered since 1851, to the effigy of the Holy Face of our Lord, exposed at Tours in the Oratory of M.

Dupont. Its date is recent, but it evidently identifies itself with the worship which Rome has rendered from time immemorial to the celebrated veil of Veronica. It continues and renews in our midst the devotion which dates from past ages in the Church; it has also given birth to a great providential work and one of evident reality- the work of reparation for blasphemies and for the profanation of Sundays, two social crimes which, at the present day, even in the very midst of Catholic nations, have assumed an extent and a degree of perversity unknown until now. It has become, through the approbation of the Head of the Church and the zeal of her clergy, the source of special benedictions and of graces of all kinds, which tend more and more to spread into the different parts of the Christian world. How striking and how worthy of remark these things are! It is always there, that miraculous picture, established in its place and venerated by M. Dupont; it is there in its modest and holy sanctuary, attracting the eyes and hearts of all; surrounded by ex-votos which increase and multiply every day; presiding over the divine mysteries celebrated continually by priests of every nation; over the nocturnal adoration of the most fervent men of the country; over regular instructions and solemn benedictions of the Blessed Sacrament; over pilgrimages brought thither by various motives from the environs or from distant countries; lastly, over a multitude of exercises and of pious works which have for their distinguishing characteristic an out-burst of the most generous love towards our Lord, and of zeal for reparation by means of His merciful Face! Before it, in that memorable spot where we have beheld it for thirty-eight years, illuminated by its crystal lamp, having at a little distance from it, as its associate and pendant, M. Dupont's Bible, also honored by a lamp, let us often, inspired by the faith of the Holy Man of Tours, repeat the prayer of the

Psalmist- Deprecatus sum Faciem tuam in toto corde meo: miserere mei secundum eloquium tuum.

THE HOLY FACE OF EDESSA

At the time when our Savior was on earth, there lived at Edessa, in Armenia, a King called Abgare. This monarch, having heard of the miracles worked by our Lord and of the holiness of his life, conceived a strong desire to have Him near to him or at least to possess his portrait. He, therefore, sent a solemn embassy to Jesus Christ. Our Lord could not leave Judea, but in order to satisfy in some measure the desire of the pious Sovereign, he took from the hands of the ambassadors a linen cloth, "a handkerchief," the tradition calls it; Himself applied it, to His Face and gave back the linen which had now become sacred, bearing as it did upon it the impress of His august Face.

King Abgare received the precious portrait with holy transports, and paid it the greatest honor. During several centuries the Holy Face of Edessa was the glory and palladium of the town, which believed that on several occasions it owed to it its deliverance and its safety. Later on, transported to Constantinople, it was obliged to be removed at the time of the Musulman invasion, that it might not be exposed to the fury of the infidels. Some Armenian Religious saved it by taking it with them to Genoa, where it is, at the present day, the object of a popular worship.

The origin and translation of this holy Picture are illustrated by miraculous legends, respecting which the most learned authors do not agree, and the authenticity of these legends has consequently never been fully attested. Therefore, spite of the respect it inspires, we cannot attach to it the same importance, or give to it the same worship that we do to the veil of Veronica preserved at St. Peter of the Vatican.

Conclusion

Rapid as have been our visits to the sanctuaries which we have described, and incomplete as have been our recitals, the result of them is, as the reader will allow, an historical fact of great importance. It is that, not only at Rome, the center of Catholicity, in the famous Vatican Basilica, but in France, at Montreuil-les-Dames, at Montreuil-sous-Laon and at Tours; in Spain, at Jaen, at Osa de la Vega and at Alicante; in Italy, at Lucca, the worship rendered to the sorrowful Face of our Lord Jesus Christ has shone for centuries with a splendor which Popes and Kings, Bishops and Magistrates have been pleased to enhance by the authority of their words and their example. Is there anything, in fact, more eminently conformable with catholic piety than to turn our eyes and our hearts towards the Face of our Lord, so unworthily outraged by sinners and yet so compassionate and merciful? The Holy Face of Jesus in His Passion has been, and will always be the symbol of suffering and of pardon; always and everywhere souls will have recourse to it in order to seek for consolation, light and strength.

That great Christian of modern times, the Holy Man of Tours, the venerable M. Dupont, was therefore really inspired by God when he asked for and received from Rome a copy of the veil of Veronica, and when he set it up in his private oratory as the standard of reparation and **a** principle of salvation. In union with the Roman Church, he felt that his devotion was true and safe; he foresaw the extension it would receive after his death, and he read with delight some of the historical notices of which we have given an abstract. He believed, and we believe with him, that the worship of the Holy Face is not new to the Church, but that it rests upon the most trustworthy and best authorized traditions.

Following his example, and walking in his footsteps, let every fervent Catholic strive to extend and to propagate this precious means of deliverance and of expiation! The events taking place at Tours, in the oratory of the Holy Face, seem prepared by Providence to revive, with respect to many different points, what is tending to become weak or to fall into desuetude; to reunite into one great whole the precious elements which are scattered abroad, and thus to form in the midst of our own age, which is in such a strange state of convulsion and rupture, a new race of Christians, a vigorous and heavenly minded generation; the one which the Prophet announced when he exclaimed- Behold the generation of them that seek the Lord, of them that seek the Face of the God of Jacob (Ps. xiii, 6).

PRAYERS

IN HONOUR OF THE HOLY FACE

BORROWED FROM

THE SOVEREIGN PONTIFFS

AND

SAINT PETER OF THE VATICAN

Prayers in Honor of the Holy Face

HYMNUS PAPAE JOANNIS XXII.

IN HONOREM SANCTAE **EFFIGIEI J.** C.[1]

Salve, sancta Facies nostri Redemptoris,
In qua nitet species divini decoris,
Impressa panniculo nivei candoris
Dataque Veronicae signum ob amoris.
Salve, decus saeculi, speculum sanctorum,
Quod videre cupiunt spiritus caelorum,

---

1. Pope John XXII, who was elected Sovereign Pontiff in **the** year 1316 **at** Avignon, composed this hymn in honor of the Holy Face, and granted an indulgence of twenty-five years and as many quarantines to whoever should recite it. He grants the same indulgence to those who, not knowing how to read, will say for the same intention five Pater, Ave and Gloria.

Nos ab omni macula purga vitiorum,
Atque nos consortio junge beatorum.
Salve, Vultus Domini, imago beata,
Ex aeterno munere mire decorata.
Lumen funde cordibus ex vi tibi data,
Et a nostris sensibus tolle colligata.
Salve, robur fidei nostrae christianae,
Destruens haereticos, qui sunt mentis vanae,
Horum auge meriturn qui te credunt sane,
Illius Effigiem qui rex fit ex pane.
Salve, nostrum gaudium in hac vita dura,
Labili et fragili, cilo peritura;
Nos deduc ad propria, o felix figura,
Ad videndam Faciem quae est Christi pura.
Salve, gemma nobilis, divina margarita,
Caelicis virtutibus perfecte munita,
Non depicta manibus, sculpta vet polita,
Hoc fit summus Pontifex, qui te fecil ita.
Ille color caelicus qui in fe splendescit,
In eodem permanet statu, nec decrescit,
Diuturno tempore minime pallescit,
Fecit te rex gloriae fallere qui nescit.
Nesciens putredinem, servans incorruptum,
Quod est a Christicolo coram te deductum,
Tu vertis in gaudium gemitum et luctum,
Confer saluberrimum te videndi fructum.
Esto nobis, quaesumus, scutum et juvamen,
Duce refrigerium atque consolamen,
Ut nobis non noceat hostile gravamen,
Sed foveamur caelicum requiem. Amen.

OREMUS

Laetifica, Domine, vultum famitiae tuae, et erue animas nostras
ex inferno inferiori, ut tui Vultus contemplatione protecti, carnis
desideria calcare valeamus, et te facie ad faciem venientum super
nos judicem securi videamus, Jesum Christum Dominum nostrum.
Amen.

HYMN OF POPE JOHN XXII

IN HONOUR OF THE HOLY FACE
Hail! Holy Face of our Redeemer, hail!
Which shines in all its majesty divine
Upon the spotless veil, a priceless gift
To Saint Veronica; of love the sign.
Hail! glory or all time, glass of the Saints,
Wherein the blessed love for aye to gaze;
Destroy within us every stain of sin,
And with th'elect our souls towards Thee raise.
Hail, Face of God! with His own girts adorned,
Whose splendor through the ages shall not cease;
Oh! make Thy light descend into our hearts,
And from their earthly toils our soul's release.
Hail! mighty bulwark of the Christian faith,
Of heresy and lies the Victor Thou;
King in the Sacred Bread, renew the strength
Of all the faithful who before Thee bow.
Hail! all our joy in this hard life below,
So frail and fugitive, so quickly o'er;
Sweet Picture, lead us onwards to the skies,
That we may there the Face or Christ adore.

Hail! noblest of nil gems, celestial pearl,

In Thee innumerable graces shine;

No hand depicted Thee, no chisel carved,

Thou wert of God alone the work divine.

The tints with which Thy features He has traced

Will never alter and will never fade;

Changeless amidst the ravages of time,

The everlasting King Thy Face has made.

For ever incorrupt and free from stain,

The living Christ we honor still in Thee;

Thou turnest into joy our sighs and tears;

Oh! grant that we, in heaven, thy Face may see.

Be thou, we pray, our buckler and defense,

Our consolation and refreshment sweet,

That nothing hostile may our spirits harm

Till; after death, we rest at Jesus' feet. Amen.

PRAYER

Shed, O Lord, joy over the faces of Thy faithful, and turn them away from the depths of hell, that, protected by the contemplation or Thy divine Face, we may have strength to trend under foot the desires or the flesh, and that we may behold Thee face to face, without fear, Lord Jesus Christ, when Thou comest to judge us. Amen.

HYMNUS PAPAE CLEMENTIS VI

IN HONOREM SANCTAE EFFIGIEI J. C. [2]

Ave, Facies praeclara,

Quae pro nobis in crucis ara,

Es facta sic pallida,

Anxietato donigrata,

Sudore sanguineo rigata,

Te texit linteola.

In quo mansit tua forma,

Quae passionis norma

Est cunctis perlucida,

Cordi meo sic impressa,

Per te, Jesu, neque cessa,

Hoc cremare indefessa

Tui amoris facula.

Post hanc vitam cum beatis,

Contemplari voluptatis

Possim Vultum deitatis,

In perenni gloria. Amen.

℣. Signatum est super nos lumen Vultus

tui, Domine;

℟. Dedisti laetitiam in corde meo.

℣. Salvum fac servum tuum,

℟. Deus meus, sperantem in te.

℣. Salvum me fac in misericordia tua, Domine;

℟. Non confundar, quoniam invocavi te.

---

2. This hymn was composed by Pope Clement VI reigning et
Avignon (France). The same Pope granted an indulgence of three
years **to** anyone reciting it before the veil of Veronica.

℣. Illumina Faciem tuam super servum tuum;

℞. Et doce roe justificationes tuas.

℣. Domine, Deus virtutum, converte nos;

℞. Et ostende Faciem tuam, et salvi erimus.

℣. Domine, exaudi orationem meam;

℞. Et clamor meus ad te veniat.

OREMUS

Deus, qui nobis signatis lumine Vultus tui, memoriale tuum instantia Veronicae imaginem tuam Sudario impressam relinquere voluisli, per passionem et crucem tuam tribue nobis, quaesumus, ita nunc in terris per speculum in aenigmate venerari, adorare, ac honorare te ipsum valeamus, ut le facic ad faciem venientem super nos judicem securi videamus, Dominum nostrum Jesum Christum. Amen.

Omnipotens sempiterne Deus, de cujus muncre praeminet haec Facies tua expressa tuo pretioso vultu, plebi tuae, quae convenit ad hanc recolendam, peccatorum suorum da veniam, et corpus, srmones, sensusque guberna, et actus eorum qui in tua pietate confidunt. Qui vivis, etc.

HYMN OF POPE CLEMENT VI.

IN HONOR OF THE HOLY FACE

O radiant Face, to Thee all hail!

For us become disfigured, pale

Upon the sacred altar rood,

All stained with drops or sweat and blood,

Thou, on the holy veil, didst trace

Its lineaments, devoid or grace.

Thy features on it thus impressed,

In testimony ever rest

Of Thy sore Passion and Thy death;

O Jesus, kindle with Thy breath,

Within my soul the flame of love,

And lift up to Thee above.

And let me, Lord, when life is o'er,

With all the blessed heavenwards soar,

And there, for aye, my longing sate,

Thy Holy Face to contemplate,

Of endless bliss the warrant sure,

Which shall from age to age endure. Amen.

℣. O Lord, Thou hast impressed upon us the light of Thy Face;

℞. Thou hast shed joy in my heart.

℣. Save Thy servant,

℞. Who hopes in Thee, O my God.

℣. Save me in Thy mercy, O Lord;

℞. That I may not have to blush for having called upon Thee.

℣. Cause the light or Thy Face to shine upon Thy servant;

℞. And teach me Thy justifications.

℣. O Lord, God of hosts, convert us;

℞. Show us Thy Face, and we shall be saved.

℣. Lord, hear my prayer;

℞. And let my cry come unto Thee.

PRAYER

O God, who host shed upon us the light of Thy Face, and who, by means or Veronica, hast willed to leave us Thy image impressed upon her veil, as an eternal warrant of Thy love, grant us, by Thy Passion and Thy Cross, grace to venerate Thee, to adore Thee and to glorify Thee now upon earth, whilst contemplating Thee as in the mirror or an enigma, in such a manner that we may not fear to look upon Thee face to face, when Thou comest Lord Jesus Christ, to judge us in the clouds of heaven. Amen.

God Eternal and Almighty, who by a special grace didst cause the precious features of Thy divine Face to shine upon Thy people assembled together to honor it, grant them the pardon of their sins, and govern the words, actions, senses and the faculties of those who confide in Thy mercy. Amen.

ORATIONES

AD SANCTAS RELIQUIAS MAJORES

Ad sanctum Sudarium beatae Veronicae.

Antiph. Tibi dixit cor meum: Quaesivi Vultum tuum; Vultum tuum, Domine, requiram: ne avertas Faciem tuam a me.

℣. Signatum est super nos lumen Vultus tui, Domine;

℟. Dedisti laetitiam in corde meo.

OREMUS

Mentibus nostris, quaesumus, Domine, Vultus sancti tui lumen benignus infunde, cujus et sapientia conditi sumus, et providentia gubernamur. Per Dominum, etc.

Ad SS. Crucem Domini Nostri Jesu Christi.

Antiph. O Crux benedicta, quae sola fuisti digna portaro Regem caelorum et Dominum.

℣. Dicite in nationibus,

℞. Quia Dominus regnavit a ligno.

OREMUS

Deus, qui unigeniti Filii tui pretioso sanguine, vivificae Crucis vexillurn sanctificare voluisti: concede, quaesumus, eos qui ejusdem sanctae Crucis gaudent honore, tua quoque ubique protectione gaudere. Per Dominum, etc.

Ad Ferrum Lanceae Domini Nostri Jesu Christi.

Antiph. Unus militum Lancea latus ejus aperuit, et continuo exivit sanguis et aqua.

℣. Lanceis vulneraverunt me;

℞. Et concussa sunt omnia ossa mea.

OREMUS

Deus qui ex tui sacri Corporis latere per Lanceam militis, sanguinem tuum in pretium, et aquam in lavacrum effudisti: concede propitius, ut qui Lanceam ipsam hic veneramur, ab omni hoste ipsius munimine protegamur. Qui vivis, etc.

PRAYERS

RECITED BEFORE THE HOLY MAJOR RELCS

Before the Holy Veil of the Blessed Veronica.

Anthem. My heart bath said to Thee- My Face
hath sought thee; Thy Face, O Lord, will I still
seek; turn not away Thy Face from me.
℣. Thou hast cast upon us the light of Thy Face, O Lord;
℞. Thou hast shed joy in my heart.

PRAYER

May Thy bounty, O Lord, shed ill our souls the sweet light of Thy
Holy Face, Thou whose wisdom has created us and whose Providence
governs us. Through our Lord Jesus Christ, etc.

Before the most Holy Cross of our Lord Jesus Christ.

Anthem. O blessed Cross, who wert alone worthy
to bear in thy arms the Lord and King of heaven.
℣. Proclaim it amongst the nations,
℞. That the Lord hath reigned through the wood of the Cross.

PRAYER

O God, who, by the precious blood of Thy **On**y begotten Son, hast
willed to sanctify the living standard of the Cross, grant, we beg of
Thee, that those who love to venerate this same holy Cross, may also
enjoy Thy powerful protection. Through our Lord Jesus Christ, etc.

Before the iron of the Lance of our Lord Jesus Christ.

Anthem. One of the soldiers opened His side
with a Lance, and there flowed forthwith blood and water.
℣. They have wounded me with their spears;
℞. And they have broken all my bones.

PRAYER

God, who from the side of Thy sacred body, pierced by the Lance of a soldier, didst shed Thy blood to redeem us and water to purify us, grant that this same Lance which we here venerate, may defend us always from our enemies. Thou who livest and reignest, etc.

Prayers to the Holy Face

Taken From the Psalms of David

My heart hath said to Thee- My face hath sought Thee; Thy Face, O Lord, will I still seek.

Turn not away Thy Face from me, decline not in Thy wrath from Thy servant.

Be Thou my helper, forsake me not; do not Thou despise me, O God my Savior. (Psalm XXXVI, 8, 9.)

Make Thy Face to shine upon Thy servant; save me in Thy mercy. (Psalm XXX, 17.)

The eyes of the Lord are upon the just: and His ears unto their prayers.

But the countenance or the Lord is against them that do evil things: to cut off the remembrance of them from the earth. (Psalm XXXIII, 16, 17.)

Why turnest Thou Thy Face away? and forgettest our want and our trouble? (Psalm XLIII, 24.)

Turn away Thy Face from my sins, and blot out all my iniquities.

Create a clean heart in me, O God: and renew a right spirit within my bowels.

Cast me not away from Thy Face; and take not Thy Holy Spirit from me. (Psalm I, 11, 12, 13.)

May God have mercy on us, and bless us: may He cause the light of His countenance to shine upon us, and may He have mercy on us.

That we may know Thy way upon earth: Thy salvation in all nations.

Let people confess to Thee, O God; let all people give praise to Thee.

Let the nations be glad and rejoice. (Psalm LXVI, 2, 3, 4, 5.)

Hear me, O Lord, for Thy mercy is kind; look upon me according to the multitude of Thy tender mercies.

And turn not away Thy Face from Thy servant; for I am in trouble, hear me speedily. (Psalm **LXVIII**, 17, 18.)

O God of hosts, convert us; and shew Thy Face, and we shall be saved. (Psalm **LXXIX**, 8.)

Turn again, O God of hosts, look down from heaven, and see, and visit this vineyard... Things set on fire and dug down shall perish at the rebuke of Thy countenance.

Let Thy hand be upon the man of Thy right hand; and upon the Son of **man** whom Thou hast confirmed for Thyself.

And we depart not from Thee, Thou shalt quicken us; and we will call upon Thy Name. (Psalm **LXXIX, 1**5, 17, 18, 19.)

O Lord, God or hosts, convert us; and shew Thy Face, and we shall be saved, (Ibid. 20.)

Behold, O God, our protector: and look on the Face of Thy Christ. (Psalm LXXIIII, 10.)

Lord, why castest Thou off my prayer, why turnest Thou away Thy Face from me? (Psalm LXXXVII, 15.)

Justice and judgment are the preparation . or Thy throne.

Mercy and truth shall go before Thy Face: blessed is the people that knoweth jubilation.

They shall walk, O Lord, in the light of Thy countenance. (Psalm LXXXIII, 15, 16.)

Hear, O Lord, my prayer, and let my cry come to Thee.

Turn not away Thy Face from me; in the day when **I** am in trouble, incline Thy ear to me.

In what day soever I shall call upon Thee, hear me speedily. (Psalm CI, 2, 3.)

I entreated Thy Face with all my heart; have mercy on me according to Thy word.

Make Thy Face to shine upon Thy servant, and teach me Thy justifications. (Psalm CXVIII, 58, 135.)

For Thy servant David's sake, turn not away Thou Face of Thy anointed.

For the Lord hath chosen Sion: He hath chosen it for His dwelling.

This is my rest forever and ever: here will I dwell for I have chosen it.

There will I bring forth a horn to David: I have prepared a lamp for my anointed. (Psalm CXXXI, 10, 13, 14, 17.)

Hear me speedily, O Lord: my spirit hath fainted away.

Turn not away Thy Face from me, lest I be like unto them that go down into the pit. (Psalm CXLII, 7.)

Promises Made by Our Lord to Those Who Worship The Holy Face

1° They shall receive upon earth an interior and constant light, and in Heaven they shall shine with a special splendor.

2° Those who contemplate the wounds or my Face upon earth shall also contemplate It irradiated with glory in Heaven.

3° Those who honor my Holy Face in a spirit or reparation will, by so doing, perform the office or St. Veronica. According to the care they take in making reparation by their homage to my Face, disfigured by blasphemers, I will, in the same degree, take care or theirs, which has been more or less disfigured by sin; My Holy Face is, as it were, the seat or the Divinity, which has the virtue or restoring in their souls the impression or the image of God.

4° Such as, by their words, prayers or writings, shall defend my cause in the work or reparation, I will defend before my Father, and I will give them my Kingdom.

5° I will sustain them.

6° I will preserve them.

7° I will assure their final perseverance.

8° By offering my Holy Face to my Father the salvation or many sinners will be obtained.

9° As, in an earthly kingdom, everything can be procured by means of a coin marked. with the effigy or the Prince, so, with the precious coin of the Holy Face, everything that can be desired will be obtained in the kingdom of Heaven.

10° By this Holy Face miracles will be worked.

OTHER FORMULAE OF PROMISES MADE BY OUR LORD TO THOSE WHO HONOR THE HOLY FACE

1° They shall receive in themselves, by the impression of My Humanity, a bright irradiation or My Divinity, and shall be so illuminated by It in their inmost souls that, by their likeness to My Face, they shall shine more than others in eternal life. (St. Gertrude, Insinuations, book IV, ch. vII).

2° St. Mechtilde having asked our Lord that those who celebrated the memory or His sweet Face, should never be deprived or His amiable company, He replied- "Not one of them shall be separated from Me." (St. Mechlilde, De la Grace Spirit., liv. I, ch. XIII).

3° "Our Lord," says Sister Marie de Saint-Pierre, "has promised me that He will imprint His divine likeness on the souls of those who honor His most holy countenance." (January 21st 1847.)

"This adorable Face is, as it were, the seal or the Divinity, which has the virtue or reproducing the likeness of God in the souls that are applied to It." (November 6th 1845.)

4° "By my Holy Face you will obtain the conversion or many sinners. Nothing that you ask in making this offering, will be refused to you. If you knew how pleasing the sight of My Face is to my Father!" *(November* 22nd 1846).

5° "As, in an earthly kingdom, you can procure all you wish with a coin marked with the Prince's effigy, so, in the kingdom of Heaven, you will obtain all you desire with the precious coin of My holy Humanity , which is My adorable countenance." (October 29th 1845.)

6° "All those who honor My Holy Face in a spirit of reparation, will, by so doing, perform the office of the pious Veronica." (*October* 27th 1845).

7° "According to the care you take in making reparation to My Face, disfigured by blasphemies, so will I take care of yours which has been disfigured by sin. I will imprint thereon My Image, and I render it as beautiful as it was on leaving the Baptismal font." *(Our* Lord *to* Sister *Marie de Saint-Pierre. November* 3rd 1845).

8° "Our Lord has promised me," says Sister Saint-Pierre, "that all those who defend His cause in this work of reparation, by words, by prayers, or in writing, He will defend before His Father; at their death, He will purify their souls by effacing all the blots of sin, and will restore to them their primitive beauty." (*March* 12th 1816).

Conditions Necessary in Order to Become An Associate

1° To be inscribed upon the Register of the Oratory of the Holy Face;

2° To receive the *rules,* with a *certificate* of admission;

3° To recite every day, for the intentions of the Archconfraternity- a Pater, Ave, Gloria, and the invocation- Domine, ostende Faciem tuam, et *salvi crimus*— "Lord, show Thy Face, and we shall he saved;"

4° To wear a picture of the Holy Face either on a cross, medal or scapular;

5° To attend as often as possible the monthly meetings;

6° To propagate the devotion to the Holy Face.

FORMULA FOR THE AGGREGATION TO
THE ARCHCONFRATERNITY OF THE HOLY FACE

By a brief of His Holiness Leo XIII, dated the 1st of October 1885, the Archconfraternity of the Holy Face was established in the Oratory of the Holy Face, at Tours, with the power of aggregating to itself, in all countries or the world , all the confraternities of the same name which, being canonically erected, desire to participate in the indulgences and other spiritual favors granted to it.

It is the Ordinary, otherwise called the Bishop of the diocese, who alone possesses the power of establishing the confraternity, or approving its statutes and rules, and of authorizing its aggregation to the archconfraternity of Tours.

The following are the three documents required by the Roman congregations-

1° An episcopal ordinance, in virtue of which the Ordinary canonically establishes the confraternity;

2° A copy of the statutes and rules, bearing the approbation and the signature or the Bishop, with the accessory modifications appropriated to the needs of the place and deemed to be suitable;

2° A testimonial Letter signed, by the Bishop and impressed with his seal, by which he authorizes the confraternity, established by him, to be aggregated to the archconfraternity at Tours.

This last document, as well as the copy of the statutes, must be sent to the director of the archconfraternity to be deposited in its archives. The ordinance of its establishment remains in the archives or the local confraternity.

Note. — 1° **We hold, at the disposition of our colleagues, two formularlcs** drawn **up in Latin,** Decretum erectionis and Litterae testimoniales, **in accordance with the formulae of the Sacred** Congregation of **Indulgences and which it is only necessary to fill up** and **sign. We** will **send them to anyone who may make application for them and they may then be submitted to the ecclesiastical authority for the purpose of abridging the labors of the secretaries.**

2° **The accessory modifications of which** our **Statutes are susceptible are applicable to Article I., which it is well to appropriate to the name of the place; - to Article VI., as regards fixing the day of the monthly meeting, and, when needful, the detail of the ceremonies; - to Article VII, where the name of the director must he indicated. - At the conclusion of Article II, there may also be added the designation of certain vices peculiar to the locality and which it is most necessary to combat or repair, for example: blasphemy,** drunkenness, **the profanation or Sunday, etc.**

According to canonical rules , it is permitted to add , but not **to suppress.**

These formalities being complied with, we then deliver to the director of the local confraternity a diploma of aggregation drawn, up in accordance with the prescriptions of the Sacred Congregations and giving a right to the indulgences and favors of the archconfraternity; at the same time, we send him a separate sheet, containing on one side the principal points of the Constitution of Clement VIII and on the other, the table or Indulgences. These documents must be preserved in the archives of the local confraternity; it will even be well to have the diploma framed.

From that time forward, it will no longer be necessary to transmit to us the names or the associates. Each confraternity, thus aggregated, has its own register, its special meetings and particular organization. The director may continue to make application to us for certificates or admission, but he signs his own name by the side of ours; or else he may use other certificates brought out by himself.

Every year, during the month of July, he must inform us of the number of associates he has received, and the condition of the confraternity of which he is director. From time to time, if the opportunity arises, he must also send us an account of the most striking ceremonies which have taken place, and of the graces which have been obtained.

It is equally requisite, indeed it is very essential, as regards the aim laid down in our statutes, and as an exterior sign of the work, that there should be in the place which is the center of the confraternity, an effigy of the Holy Face, similar to that or the Oratory at Tours, which is an authentic *fac*-simile of the veil of St. Veronica. It should be publicly exposed in a suitable place and decorated in the manner most likely to excite the piety of the faithful, and it should be, as frequently as possible, accompanied by a lamp, lighted night and day, as a sign of honor and of reparation.

N. B. - These directions will be useful to ecclesiastics and even to laymen who, in concert with their pastors, are occupied in establishing or aggregating a confraternity. The two formulae: the Ordinance of establishment and the Testimonial letter, printed in accordance with **the Roman instructions, can be sent to them in order to be submitted to the secretary or the Bishop, when there wlll be nothing more to do than to fill them up.**

The price of each sheet is 2d.[1]/2. — *Expense of the Diploma and of the sheet annexed to it: 1s.* 8d. - *Voluntary offering which, including the above expense, must not,* in *conformity with the constitutions of Clement* VIII., *exceed* £ 1. 4. 2.

In certain places in which the confraternity of the Holy Face has been established, an excellent custom has been introduced, which we commend highly. Besides the official director named by the Bishop there is a lady president of the work assisted by one or two counsellors and some zealous persons, who form a little council under the authority of the ecclesiastical director, who may be of great use to him in particular cases relative to the

confraternity. This means has evidently precious advantages. But it is quite optional with the director to adopt it or not. Should any director choose to employ it, he will without doubt find in his parish a sufficient number of devote and generous souls, as providentially they are to be found in every parish.

DIPLOMA OF UNION. - Under the title of "Diploma of Union or prayers and of merits," letters of affiliation may be granted to parishes, to communities, to associations and to other pious institutions, which, not possessing a confraternity, desire nevertheless to be united to us by a special link and cooperate in the work of reparation of the Holy Face. This diploma of union, differing from the diploma of aggregation, does not give a right to the indulgences, but it confers a **participation in the prayers, adorations,** merits and good works of the whole archconfraternity.

As an exception and a privilege denoting a specially distinguished favor, the diploma of union may be granted to certain zelators or benefactors who have rendered important services to the work or the Holy Face.

In these special cases, no canonical formality is required for their reception.

NOTICES

The Holy Sacrifice of the mass- Daily at 6, 7 and 8 o'clock.

Recitation of the Litany of the Holy Face with recommendations and prayers- Daily, in the morning after the 7 o'clock mass, and in the evening at 5 o'clock.

Monthly meeting of the Archconfraternity of the Holy Face- On the last Sunday or the month at 5 o'clock in the evening; instruction and Benediction.

The Way of the Cross- On the second Friday of the month at 5 o'clock in the evening.

Nocturnal Adoration- Every Tuesday evening, from 9:30pm to 5 o'clock on Wednesday morning.

Diurnal Adoration- Every Wednesday , from 5 o'clock in the morning to 5 o'clock in the evening, concluded with instruction and Benediction.

Pilgrimages of Reparation- Every year, from Palm Sunday to Good Friday.

Mr. Dupont's mortuary room- May be visited at every hour in the day.

Offering of candles- From 2d. ½ to 10d.

Lighted Lamp- For a novena, 2s. fid.; for a month, 8s., and for a year £ 2. 8. 0.

Oil of the Holy Face- Sent in a box by post. Price- is. 3d.

Intentions for Masses- In consequence or the expense or the work, the offering for each mass required at the Oratory is 18. 8d., of which 5d. is appropriated to the work.

The chaplets, medals of St. Benedict and other articles forwarded from the Oratory receive the blessings and Indulgences suitable to them, and do not lose them by being gratuitously distributed.

Correspondence- Letters to be prepaid, and a Postage.-stamp enclosed if an answer be required. Address to be legibly written and the railway station specified to which articles are to be sent. Address- M. l'abbe Celestin Balsiau, Directeur des Pretres de la Sainte-Face, rue Bernard-Palissy, 8, Tours (France).

The Oratory is open to foreign pilgrims everyday, from 5:30 in the morning to 6:30 in the evening: Two confessionals are placed at their disposal.

Recommendations may be sent by post, or entered in a book kept for the purpose in the vestibule of the Oratory.

Persons are earnestly requested to notify in writing any graces received and also to have ex-voto, put up in token of thankfulness.